BY THE SAME AUTHOR

True and False Democracy—Charles Scribner's Sons
(First Edition, The Macmillan Co., 1907)—xii +
111 pp. . . . . . . *net* 75 cents

The American as He Is—Charles Scribner's Sons
(First Edition, The Macmillan Co., 1908)—x +
97 pp. . . . . . . *net* 75 cents

Philosophy—Columbia University Press, 1911—vii +
51 pp. . . . . *net* $1.00

**Why Should We Change Our Form of Govern-
ment ?**—Charles Scribner's Sons, 1912—xv +
159 pp. . . . . . . *net* 75 cents

The International Mind—Charles Scribner's Sons,
1913—x + 121 pp. . . . *net* 75 cents

The Meaning of Education—Charles Scribner's Sons,
1915—xiii + 385 pp. . . . *net* $1.50

A WORLD IN FERMENT

INTERPRETATIONS OF THE WAR
FOR A NEW WORLD

A WORLD IN FERMENT

INTERPRETATIONS OF THE WAR
FOR A NEW WORLD

BY

NICHOLAS MURRAY BUTLER

PRESIDENT OF COLUMBIA UNIVERSITY
MEMBER OF THE AMERICAN ACADEMY OF ARTS AND LETTERS

NEW YORK

CHARLES SCRIBNER'S SONS

1918

TO THOSE MEN AND WOMEN OF WHATEVER
LAND WHO PRIZE INDIVIDUAL LIBERTY, WHO
DISTINGUISH TRUE DEMOCRACY FROM FALSE,
AND WHO WISH TO LIVE IN A WORLD WHICH IS
AT PEACE BECAUSE IT IS BOTH FREE AND JUST

CONTENTS

CONTENTS

I

INTRODUCTION

INTRODUCTION

Since August 1, 1914, no American has been quite free to speak in public on the issues and the consequences of the war without bearing constantly in mind the attitude of the Government of the United States. That attitude, which began as neutrality and which on April 6, 1917 passed over into participation in the conflict, has in its various stages of development probably marked with substantial correctness the state of American public opinion in relation to the war. When one looks back, however, from participation to neutrality, he cannot help seeing how imperfectly, even from the very beginning, neutrality reflected the actual relations of the war to the present and the future of the people of the United States. Nevertheless, it takes time and events of a compelling character to affect the controlling opinion of a nation of more than one hundred millions whose traditions are of detachment from world politics in general and from European controversies in particular. It seems quite certain that the future historian will dwell with more emphasis upon the complete transformation which the war has effected in the feelings and policies of the people of the United States than upon the fact that it took nearly three years to effect that transformation.

It may well be that the war would have been differently conducted and more quickly ended had the Government of the United States announced immediately on the first declaration of war that, as a co-signatory of the Hague Conventions, it would deem it a duty to protest against the violation by any belligerent of the Hague Conventions, of the laws and customs of civilized warfare, or of the rules of international law. Such a declaration would not have prevented the invasion of Belgium; that had been planned too long and was too essential a part of the contemplated attack to be so easily checked. But it might well have prevented some of the shocking outrages that followed in Belgium, in northern France, in Poland, in Serbia, and in Roumania, as well as have held in leash the dogs of submarine warfare. Whether this be true or not, such a declaration would have marked an epoch in the history of nations, for it would have pointed

with the utmost energy and directness to law
at a time when resort to force was being had
on a scale hitherto unheard of in history.

As the war has proceeded, it has become so
plain that even he who runs may read, that it
is essentially a war for a new world. It is a
war for a new international world, and a war
for a new intranational world.

It requires no great gift of prophecy to fore-
see that the new international world that will
almost certainly arise upon the ruins of this war
will be one in which the nations of the earth
will band themselves together more closely than
ever before, not to enforce peace but to secure peace. The dreams of seers and the long-
cherished projects of statesmen are likely soon
to be fulfilled in many of their essential parts.
This appears to be a safe prediction, for the
reason that there seems to be no other way in
which human foresight and human capacity
can make highly improbable the recurrence of
any such holocaust as is now consuming civilization. Some suggestions as to ways and means
by which this new international world may be
achieved and established are offered in the
pages that follow.

The war is also a war for a new intranational world. The political developments in Great Britain, in France, and in the United States, to say nothing of the stupendous revolution in Russia, indicate the character of this new world. It will be a world in which democracy will be more secure, more effective, more just and better established. It is to be hoped that it will be a world in which there will be a larger measure of co-operation between government and private enterprise than has heretofore been usual, but in which government will not stifle and suppress private enterprise with its clumsy and costly hand. It will not be a world from which vagaries and vice can be excluded, because vagaries and vice accompany humanity on its progress; but there is every reason to believe that it will be a world purified and strengthened by the tremendous trials to which the world of to-day is being subjected.

The new world will be one in which international policies will play a greatly increased part. Perhaps the greatest enemy of true internationalism is false internationalism. Movements to advance international interdependence and international understanding are of two distinct kinds. One of these is both misleading and harmful, and by its methods and processes would make the achievement of its declared aim quite impossible. The other is wise and statesmanlike, and follows the path by which such progress as has already been made has been achieved. Of these two methods of promoting what may be called internationalism the former would proceed by denouncing all nationalistic and patriotic feeling whatsoever in order to exalt the supernational brotherhood of man, and to lay stress upon a world-wide community without national ties or national ambitions. To use a figure drawn from chemistry, this might be called colloidal internationalism. It is hopelessly impractical as an ideal, and hopelessly unsound and unstable as a public policy, whether for individuals or for nations. The second method of promoting internationalism would strengthen and develop nationalistic and patriotic sentiments and aims, in order that when so strengthened they may be used without impairment or weakening as elements in a larger human undertaking of which each nation should be an independent and integral part. Pursuing the same figure, this might be called crystalline internationalism. The strength and beauty of the whole international structure when complete would then depend upon and reflect the strength and beauty of each of its national elements. The colloidal internationalism of the type of person who insists that he knows no country but humanity, and that he is a citizen of no state but only of the world, is hopeless nonsense. It prevents the development of true internationalism by affronting common sense.

It is hoped that the new world will also come to an understanding with itself about peace. It will perhaps understand, what some excellent persons are not now able to see, that peace is not an ideal at all; it is a state attendant upon the achievement of an ideal. The ideal itself is human liberty, justice, and the honorable conduct of an orderly and humane society. Given this, a durable peace follows naturally as a matter of course. Without this, there is no peace, but only a rule of force until liberty and justice revolt against it in search of peace. It is Tacitus who records the British chieftain Calgacus as saying of the invading Romans of his day, *Solitudinem faciunt, pacem appellant.* If *Imperium* be read for *Solitudinem*, this pregnant sentence is a true description of the political philosophy and the military policy of the twentieth century Teutons.

To regard peace as an end in itself and as something to be achieved at all hazards, is in effect to labor for the indefinite continuance of war. The new world of which we are in search will insist upon justice, liberty, and righteousness. as its foundation, and it will welcome durable peace as their accustomed companion and friend.

NICHOLAS MURRAY BUTLER.

COLUMBIA UNIVERSITY
In the City of New York
July 14, 1917

II

THE ONRUSH OF WAR

An Address at the Opening of the 161st Academic Year
of Columbia University, September 23, 1914

THE ONRUSH OF WAR

Our usual interests however great, our usual problems however pressing, all seem petty and insignificant in view of what has befallen the world while we were seeking rest and refreshment in the summer holiday. The murky clouds of cruel, relentless war, lit by the lightning flash of great guns and made more terrible by the thunderous booming of cannon, hang over the European countries that we know and love so well. The great scholars that we would have so gladly welcomed here, have not come to us. They are killing and being killed across the sea. Friends and colleagues whom we honor are filled with hate toward each other, and toward each other's countrymen. The words that oftenest come to our lips, the ideals that we cherish and pursue, the progress that we fancied we were making, seem not to exist. Mankind is back in the primeval forest, with the elemental brute passions finding a truly fiendish expression. The only apparent use of science is to enable men to kill other men more quickly and in greater numbers. The only apparent service of philosophy is to make the worse appear the better reason. The only apparent evidence of the existence of religion is the fact that divergent and impious appeals to a palpably pagan God, have led him, in perplexed distress, to turn over the affairs of Europe to an active and singularly accomplished devil.

What are we to think? Is science a sham? Is philosophy a pretense? Is religion a mere rumor? Is the great international structure of friendship, good will, and scholarly co-operation upon which this University and many of its members have worked so long, so faithfully, and apparently with so much success, only an illusion? Are the long and devoted labors of scholars and of statesmen to enthrone Justice in the place of Brute Force in the world, all without effect? Are Lowell's lines true—

> "Right forever on the scaffold,
> Wrong forever on the throne"?

The answer is No; a thousand times, No!

Despite all appearances, even in this wicked and unprovoked assault on the liberties of

peace-loving men and nations which is decimat-
ing the flower of European manhood, multiply-
ing by the million the widows, the orphans, the
suffering, and the distressed, wrecking the commercial and industrial progress of a century,
impoverishing alike the belligerents and the
neutrals, closing the exchanges from New York
to Buenos Aires, ruining the cotton-planter of
the South as well as the copper-miner of the
Far West, loosing in the frenzied combatants
the primitive instincts of savagery and lust—
even here there is to be found something on
which this University may continue to build
the temple of wisdom, of justice, and of true
civilization to which its hand was laid when
George II was king, when Louis XV still reigned
in France, and when Frederick the Great was
at the height of his fame in Prussia.

We are a neutral nation, and the President
has enjoined us all to observe neutrality in
speech and in deed; but neutrality is not indifference. Ours is not the neutrality of the
casual passer-by who views with amused care-
lessness a fight between two street rowdies; it is
the neutrality of the just judge who aims, without passion and without prejudice, to render

judgment on the proved facts. We cannot if we would refrain from passing judgment upon the conduct of men, whether singly or in nations, and we should not attempt to do so.

In the first place, the moral judgment of the American people as to the aggressors in this war and as to the several steps in the declaration and conduct of it, is clear, calm, and practically unanimous. There is no beating of drums and blowing of bugles, but rather a sad pain and grief that our kin across the sea, owing whatever allegiance and speaking whatever tongue, have been led to engage in public murder and destruction on the most stupendous scale recorded in history. This of itself proves that the education of public opinion has proceeded far, and, whatever he who extols war for its own sake may say, it shows that the heart of the American people is sound and its head well-informed. The attitude of the American press is worthy of the highest praise; in some notable instances the very high-water mark of dignity and of power has been reached. When the war-clouds have lifted, I believe that the moral judgment of the American people as to the responsibility for this war will prove to be that of the sober-minded and fair-minded men in every country of Europe.

Next, it must not be forgotten that this war was made primarily by kings and by cabinets; it was not decreed by peoples. We can all testify that the statement that kings and cabinets were forced into the war by public sentiment is absolutely untrue so far at least as several of the belligerent nations are concerned. Certainly in not more than two cases were the chosen representatives of the people consulted at all. A tiny minority in each of several countries whose conduct was hostile and provoked hostilities may have desired war, but the militarist spirit was singularly lacking among the masses of the population in Germany, in Austria-Hungary, and in Russia. There the people generally have simply accepted with grim resignation and reluctant enthusiasm the conflict which in each case they are taught to believe has been forced on them by another's aggression.

The most significant statement that I heard in Europe was made to me on the third day of August last by a German-speaking railway servant, a grizzled veteran of the Franco-Prussian War. In reply to my question as to whether he would have to go to the front, the old man said: "No; I am too old. I am seventy-two. But my four boys went yesterday, God help them! and I hate to have them go. For, sir," he added in a lowered voice, "this is not a people's war; it is a kings' war, and when it is over there may not be so many kings."

Again, a final end has now been put to the contention, always made with more emphasis than reasonableness, that huge armaments are themselves an insurance against war and an aid in maintaining peace. This argument was invented by those who really believe in war and in armaments as ends in themselves. Sundry politicians, many newspapers, and not a few good people who are proud to have their thinking done for them, accepted this dictum as a profound political truth. Its falsity is now plain to every one. Guns and bullets and armor are not made to take the place of postage stamps and books and laboratories and other instruments of civilization and of peace; they are made to kill people. Their only other possible use is to excite terror, and terror, national or international, is not a safe foundation on which to attempt to build a civilization.

It seems pretty clear that when the present huge supplies of guns and ammunition are used up in the contest now going on, no civilized people will ever again permit its government to enter into a competitive armament race. The time may not be so very far distant when to be the first moral power in the world will be a considerably greater distinction than to be the first military power or the first naval power, and when the several nations will band themselves together to repress the rule of force and to advance the rule of law. How any one, not a fit subject for a madhouse, can find in the awful events now happening in Europe a reason for asking the United States to desist from its attempts to promote a new international order in the world, is to me wholly inconceivable.

Another great gain is to be found in the fact that no one is willing to be responsible for this war. Every combatant alleges that he is on the defensive, and summons his fellow countrymen who are scientists and philosophers to find some way to prove it. The old claim that war was a part of the moral order, a God-given instrument for the spreading of enlightenment,

and the only real training-school for the manly
virtues, is just now in a state of eclipse. Each
one of the several belligerent nations insists
that it—and its government—are devoted
friends of peace, and that it is at war only because war was forced upon it by the acts of
some one else. As to who that some one else
is, it has not yet been possible to get a unanimous agreement. What we do know is that
no one steps forward to claim credit for the
war or to ask a vote of thanks or a decoration
for having forced it upon Europe and upon the
world. Everybody concerned is ashamed of it
and apologetic for it.

It may well be, moreover, that the desper-
ately practical and direct education which this
war is already affording will hasten very much
the coming of the day when the close economic
and intellectual interdependence of the nations
will assert itself more emphatically and more
successfully against national chauvinism and
the preposterous tyranny of those who worship
at the shrine of militarism. The armed peace
which preceded this war and led directly to it,
was in some respects worse than war itself; for
it had many of the evils of war without war's

educational advantages. We are not likely to return again to that form of wickedness and folly, unless perchance the continent of Europe is able to produce another generation of public men as self-centred and of as narrow a vision as those who have generally been in control of public policy there for forty years past. The whole card-house of alliances and ententes, together with the balance of power theory, has come tumbling heavily to the ground. Something far different and much more rational will arise in its stead. In the Europe of to-morrow there will be no place for secret treaties and understandings, for huge systems of armed camps and limitless navies, for wide-spread international enmity and treachery, for carefully stimulated race and religious hatred, or for wars made on the sole responsibility of monarchs and of ministers. Moral, social, and political progress will refuse longer to pay the crushing tolls which a conventional diplomacy and an unenlightened statesmanship have demanded of them. It is not the Slav or the Teuton, the Latin or the Briton, the Oriental or the American, who is the enemy of civilization and of culture. Militarism, there is the enemy!

The first notable victim of the Great War was the eloquent and accomplished French parliamentarian, M. Jaurès. He was murdered by a war-crazed fanatic. In the course of a long and intimate conversation with M. Jaurès shortly before his tragic death, he dwelt much on the part that America could play in binding the nations of Europe together. He spoke of the success of the policies that had been worked out here to make the United States and Germany and the United States and France better known to each other, and he thought that through the agency of the United States it might eventually be practicable to draw Germany and France together in real trust and friendship. As we parted, his last words to me were: "Do not leave off trying. No matter what the difficulties are, do not leave off trying." To-day the words of this great socialist leader of men seem like a voice from beyond the grave. They are true. We must not leave off trying.

When exhaustion, physical and economic, brings this war to an end, as I believe it must, the task of America and Americans will be heavy and responsible. It will be for us to bind up the war's wounds, to soften the war's animosities, and to lead the way in the colossal work of reconstruction that must follow. Then if our heads are clear, our hearts strong, and our aims unselfish—and if our nation continues to show that it means always to keep its own plighted word—we may gain new honor and imperishable fame for our country. We may yet live to see our great policies of peace, of freedom from entangling alliances, of a world concert instead of a continental balance of power, of an international judiciary and an international police, of international co-operation instead of international suspicion, generally assented to, and, as a result, the world's resources set free to improve the lot of peoples, to advance science and scholarship, and to raise humanity to a level yet unheard of. Here lies the path of national glory for us, and here is the call to action in the near future.

It is often darkest just before the dawn, and the hope of mankind may lie in a direction other than that Europe toward which we are now looking so anxiously. Arthur Hugh Clough's noble verses are an inspiration to us at this hour:

" Say not the struggle naught availeth,
    The labour and the wounds are vain,
The enemy faints not, nor faileth,
    And as things have been they remain.

*   *   *   *   *   *   *

For while the tired waves, vainly breaking,
    Seem here no painful inch to gain,
Far back, through creeks and inlets making,
    Comes silent, flooding in, the main.

And not by eastern windows only,
    When daylight comes, comes in the light;
In front the sun climbs slow, how slowly!
    But westward, look, the land is bright!"

III

THE UNITED STATES OF EUROPE

An Interview with Edward Marshall printed in the New York *Times*, October 18, 1914

THE UNITED STATES OF EUROPE

What will be in substance a United States of Europe, a more or less formal federation of the self-governing countries of Europe, may be the outcome of the demonstrated failure of the existing national system to adjust government to the growth of civilization. The ending of the present war may see the rising of the sun of democracy to light a new day of freedom even for those of our transatlantic neighbors who now seem most remote from it.

Thinking men in all the contending nations are beginning seriously to consider such a contingency, to argue for it or against it; in other words, to regard it as an undoubted possibility.

The European cataclysm puts the people of the United States in a unique and tremendously important position. As neutrals we are able to observe events and to learn the lessons that they teach. If we learn rightly we may gain for ourselves and be able to confer upon others benefits far more important than any of the material advantages which may come to us through a shrewd handling of the new possibilities in international trade.

Prophecy is always hazardous, and never more so than now, but it seems clear that the world is at the crossroads and that everything may depend upon the United States, which has been thrust by events into a unique position of moral leadership. Whether the march of the future is to be to the right or to the left, up hill or down, after the war is over, may well depend upon the course this nation shall now take, and upon the influence which it shall exercise. If we keep our heads clear there are two things that we can bring insistently to the attention of Europe—each of vast import at such a time as that which will follow the ending of the war.

The first of these is the fact that race antagonisms tend to die away and disappear under the influence of liberal and enlightened political institutions. This has been proved in the United States. We have huge Celtic, Latin, Teutonic, and Slavonic populations all living here at peace and in harmony; and as years pass they tend to merge, creating new and homogeneous types. The Old World antagonisms have become memories. This proves that such antagonisms are not mysterious attributes of geography or of climate, but that they are the outgrowth chiefly of social and political conditions. Here a man can do about what he likes, so long as he does not violate the law; he may pray as he pleases or not at all, and he may speak any language that he chooses. The United States is itself proof that most of the contentions of Europeans as to race antagonisms are ill-founded. We have demonstrated that racial antagonisms need not necessarily become the basis of permanent hatred and an excuse for war.

If human beings are given the chance they will make the most of themselves, and by living happily—which means living in justice and at peace—they will avoid conflict. The hyphen tends to disappear from American terminology. The German-American, the Italo-American, the Irish-American all become Americans. So, by and large, our institutions have proved their capacity to amalgamate and to set free every type of human being which thus far has come under our flag. There is in this a lesson which may well be taken seriously to heart by the leaders of opinion in Europe when this war ends.

The second thing which we may with propriety press upon the attention of the people of Europe after peace comes to them, is the fact that we are not only the great exponents, but the great example, of the success of the principle of federation as a basis of unity in political life regardless of local, economic, and racial differences. If our fathers had attempted to organize this country upon the basis of a single, closely unified State, it would have gone to smash almost at the outset, wrecked by clashing economic and personal interests. Indeed, this nearly happened in the civil war, which was more economic than political in its origin. But, though we had our difficulties, we did find a way to make a unified nation of a hundred million people and forty-eight commonwealths, all bound together in unity and in loyalty to a common political ideal and a common political purpose. Why is not this principle of federation, not in all its details but in its fundamentals, applicable to a group of European States that wish to achieve a common purpose?

There might readily be a federation into the United States of Europe.

When one nation sets out to assert itself by force against the will, or even the wish, of its neighbors, disaster must inevitably come. Disaster would have come here if, in 1789, New York had endeavored to assert itself against New England or Pennsylvania. As a matter of fact certain inhabitants of Rhode Island and of Pennsylvania did try something of the sort after the Federal Government had been formed, but, fortunately, their effort was a failure. The leaders of our national life had established so flexible and so admirable a plan of government that it was soon apparent that each State could retain its identity, form its own ideals and shape its own progress, and still remain a loyal part of the whole nation; that each State could make a place for itself in the new federation and not be destroyed thereby.

There is no reason why each nation in Europe should not make a place for itself in the sun of unity which I feel sure is rising there behind the war-clouds. Europe's stupendous economic loss, which already has been appalling and will soon be incalculable, will give us an opportunity to press this argument home.

True internationalism is not the enemy of the nationalistic principle. On the contrary, it helps true nationalism to thrive. The Vermonter is more a Vermonter because he is an American, and there is no reason why Hungary, for example, should not be more than ever before Hungarian after it becomes a member of the United States of Europe.

Europe, of course, is not without examples of the successful application of the principle of federation within itself. It so happens that the federated State next greatest to our own is the German Empire. It is only forty-three years old, but there federation has been notably successful. The idea of federation is perfectly familiar to German publicists.

It is familiar, also, to the English, and has lately been pressed as the probable final solution of the Irish question. It has insistently suggested itself as the solution of the Balkan problem. In a lesser way it already is represented in the structure of Austria-Hungary. This principle of nation-building, of international building through federation, certainly has in it the seeds of the world's next great development—and we Americans are in a position both to expound the theory and to illustrate the practice. This may be the greatest work which America will have to do at the end of this war.

The cataclysm is so awful that it is quite within the bounds of truth to say that the world can never again be the same as it was. This conflict is the birth-throe of a new European order of things. The man who attempts to judge the future by the old standards or to force the future back to them will be found to be hopelessly out of date. The world will have no use for him. The world has left behind forever the international policies of Palmerston and of Beaconsfield and even those of Bismarck, which were far more powerful. When the war ends, conditions will be such that a new kind of imagination and a new kind of statesmanship will be required. This war will prove to be the most effective education of 500,000,000 people which could possibly have been thought of, although it is the most costly and most terrible means which could have been chosen. The results of this education will be shown in the process of general reconstruction which will doubtless follow.

All the talk of which so much is heard about the peril from the Slav or from the Teuton or from the Celt is unworthy of serious attention. It would be quite as reasonable to discuss seriously the red-headed peril or the six-footer peril. There is no peril to the world in the Slav, the Teuton, the Celt, or any other race, provided the people of that race have an opportunity to develop as social and economic units, and are not so bound and confined by tyranny as to force an explosion, or so deluded by militarism and national chauvinism as to become a public danger. It is not races but wrong ideas that are dangerous.

No form of government will long be tolerated which does not set men free to develop in their own way.

The international organization of the world already has progressed much farther than is ordinarily understood. Ever since the Franco-Prussian war and the Geneva Arbitration, both landmarks in modern history, this organization has advanced inconspicuously, but by leaps and bounds. The postal service of the world has been internationalized in its control for years. The several Postal Conventions have given evidences of an international administrative organization of the highest order. Europe abounds in illustrations of the international administration of large things. The very laws of war, which are at present the subject of so much and such bitter discussion, are the result of international organization. They were not adopted by a Congress, a Parliament, or a Reichstag. They were agreed to by many and divergent peoples, who sent representatives to meet for their discussion and determination. In the admiralty law we have a most striking example of uniformity of practice in all parts of the world. If a ship is captured or harmed in the Far East and taken into Yokohama or Nagasaki, damages will be assessed and collected precisely as they would be in New York or Liverpool. The world is gradually developing a code for international legal procedure. Special arbitral tribunals have tended to merge and to grow into the international court at The Hague, and that in turn will develop until it becomes a real supreme judicial tribunal.

Of course the analogy between the federated State and a federation of nations fails at some points, but the time will come when each nation will deposit in a world federation some portion of its sovereignty for the general good. When this happens it will be possible to establish an international executive and an international police, both devised for the especial purpose of enforcing the decisions of the international court.

Here, again, the United States offers a perfect object-lesson. Its central government is one of limited and defined powers. Its history can show Europe how such limitations and definitions may be established and interpreted, and how they may be modified and amended when necessary to meet new conditions. There will be annotated reports of the decisions of the several international arbitration tribunals and of the international court of justice, in order that the governments and jurists of the world may have at hand, as they have in the United States Supreme Court reports, a record of decided cases, which, when the time comes, may be referred to as precedents. It will be through gradual processes such as these that the great end will be accomplished. Beginning with such annotated reports as a basis for precedents, each new case tried before this tribunal will add a farther precedent, and presently a complete international code will be in existence. It was in this way that the English common law was built, and such has been the history of the admirable work done by our own judicial system. The study of such problems as these is at this time infinitely more important than the consideration of how large a fine shall be inflicted by the victors upon the vanquished.

There is the probability of some dislocation of territory and some shiftings of sovereignty after the war ends, but these will be of comparatively minor importance.

Dislocation of territory and the shifting of sovereigns as the result of international disagreements are mediæval practices. After this war the world will want to solve its problems in terms of the future, not in those of the outgrown past. The important result of this great war will be the stimulation of international organization along some such lines as those suggested.

Conventional diplomacy and conventional statesmanship have very evidently broken down in Europe. They have made a disastrous failure of the work with which they were intrusted. They did not and could not prevent the war because they knew and used only the old formulas. They had no tools for a job like this. A new type of international statesman is certain to arise, a statesman who will have a grasp of new tendencies, a new outlook upon life. Bismarck used to say that it would pay any nation to wear the clean linen of a civilized State. The truth of this must be taught to those nations of the world which are weakest in morale, and it can only be done as similar work is accomplished with individuals. Courts, not killings, have accomplished it with individuals.

One more point ought to be remembered. We sometimes hear it said that nationalism, the desire for national expression by each individual nation, makes the permanent peace and good order of the world impossible. It seems absurd to believe that this is any truer of nations than it is of individuals. It is not each nation's desire for national expression which makes peace impossible; it is the fact that thus far in the world's history such desire has been bound up with militarism. The nation whose frontier bristles with bayonets and with forts is like the individual with a magazine pistol in his pocket. Both make for murder. Both in their hearts really mean murder. The world will be better when the nations invite the judgment of their neighbors and are influenced by it. When John Hay said that the Golden Rule and the Open Door should guide our new diplomacy, he said something which should be applicable to the new diplomacy of the whole world. The Golden Rule and a free chance are all that any man ought to want or ought to have, and they are all that any nation ought to want or ought to have.

One of the controlling principles of a democratic State is that its military and naval establishments must be completely subservient to the civil power. They should form the police, and not be the dominant factor of any nation's life. As soon as they go beyond this simple function in any nation, then that nation is afflicted with militarism.

It is difficult to make predictions as to the

war's effect on us. Our position will depend a good deal upon the outcome of the conflict, and what that will be no one at present can tell. If a new map of Europe follows the war, its permanence will depend upon whether or not the changes are such as will permit nationalities to organize as nations. The world should have learned through the lessons of the past that it is impossible permanently and peacefully to submerge large bodies of aliens if they are treated as aliens. That is the opposite of the mixing process which is still building a nation out of varied nationalities in the United States. The old Romans understood this. They permitted their outlying vassal nations to speak any language they chose and to worship whatever god they chose, so long as they recognized the sovereignty of Rome. When a conquering nation goes beyond that and begins to suppress religions, languages, and customs, it also begins, at that very moment, to sow the seeds of insurrection and revolution.

A true nation has been defined as an ethnographic unit inhabiting a geographic unit. That is an illuminating definition. If a nation

is not an ethnographic unit, it tries to become
one by oppressing or amalgamating the weaker
portions of its people. If it is not a geographic
unit, it tries to become one by reaching out to
a mountain chain or to the sea—to something
which will serve as a real dividing-line between
it and its next neighbors. The accuracy of
this definition can hardly be denied, and we
all know what the violations of this principle
have been in Europe. It is unnecessary to
point them out.

Races rarely have been successfully mixed
by conquest. The military victor in a war is
not always the real conqueror in the long run.
The Normans conquered Saxon England, but
Saxon law and Saxon institutions worked up
through the new power and have dominated
England's later history. The Teutonic tribes
conquered Rome, but Roman civilization, by
a sort of capillary attraction, went up into the
mass above and presently dominated the Teutons. The persistency of a civilization may
well be superior in tenacity to mere military
conquest and control.

The smallness of the number of instances in
which conquering nations have been able suc-

cessfully to deal with alien peoples is extraordinary. The Romans were usually successful, and England has been successful with all but the Irish; but perhaps no other peoples have been successful in high degree in an effort to hold alien populations as vassals or as fellow subjects and to make them really happy and comfortable as such.

One of the war's chief effects on us will be to change our point of view. Europe will be more vivid to us from now on. There are many American public men who have never thought much about Europe, and who have been far from a realization of its actual importance to us. It has been a place in which to pass a summer holiday. But suddenly Americans find they cannot sell their cotton in Europe or their copper, that they cannot market their stocks and bonds there, that they cannot send money to their families who are travelling there, because there is a war. To such men the war must have made it apparent that interdependence among nations is more than a mere phrase. Our entire trade and all our economic and social policies must recognize this fact. The world has discovered that money without credit means little. One cannot use money if one cannot use one's credit to draw it whenever and wherever needed. Credit is intangible and volatile, and may be destroyed overnight. International credit implies national interdependence.

This realization of national interdependence will elevate and refine our patriotism by teaching men a wider sympathy and a deeper understanding of other peoples, nations, and languages. I sincerely hope it will educate us up to what I have called "the international mind."

There are hopeful signs, even in the midst of the gloom that hangs over us. Think what it has meant for the great nations of Europe to come to us, as they have done, asking our favorable public opinion. We have no army and no navy worthy of their fears. They can have been induced by nothing save their conviction that we are the possessors of sound political ideals and are a great moral force in the world. In other words, they do not now want us to fight for them, but they do want us to approve of them. They want us to pass judgment upon the humanity and the legality of their acts, because they feel that our judgment will be the judgment of history. There is a lesson in this.

If we had not repealed the Panama Canal Tolls Exemption act in June, 1914, the European nations might not have come to us as they are doing now. Who would have cared for our opinion in the matter of a treaty violation if, for mere financial interest or from sheer vanity, we ourselves had violated a solemn treaty? When Congress repealed the Panama Canal Tolls Exemption act it marked an epoch in the history of the United States. This did more than the Spanish War, more than the building of the Panama Canal or than anything else I can think of to make us a true world power. As a nation we have kept our word when sorely tempted to break it. We made Cuba independent, we have not exploited the Philippines, we have stood by our word as to Panama Canal tolls.

In consequence we are the first moral power in the world to-day. Others may be first with armies, still others first with navies. But we have made good our right to be appealed to on questions of national and international morality. That Europe is seeking our favor is the acknowledgment of this fact by the European nations and their tribute to it.

IV

THE UNITED STATES AS A WORLD POWER

An Interview with Edward Marshall printed in the
New York *Times*, May 16, 1915

THE UNITED STATES AS A WORLD POWER

When one speaks of the United States as a world power, and of its future opportunities as such, one must stop to ask whether he is using the term "world power" in the military sense with reference to the rule of force, or in the moral sense with reference to the rule of ideals and of law. The history of the world makes it pretty plain that there is a distinction between the two.

Our present-day philosophy of life makes it equally plain that it is world power resting on ideals and on law that the United States should aim at—the world power of the future—and not the sort of world power which rests on force—the world power of the past. With the passing of the years, with the increase in area and the multiplication of population, the United States has become at once the largest, the richest, and the most powerful exemplar of democratic institutions on the globe. Any claim which it may have to being a world

power to-day and any hope which it may have
of increasing or extending this world power in
future must rest upon its being true to the
ideals and aims of democracy, not only in form
but in spirit and in fact. The very just in-
dignation of the American people at the destruction of the *Lusitania*, involving, as it did,
the loss of hundreds of lives of neutrals and
non-combatants, including many women and
children, as well as the inexplicable attack
upon the American ship *Gulflight*, only emphasize the necessity of maintaining our purpose
to enforce the rights which attach to neutrals.
To do this successfully will of itself be a manifestation of world power on a great scale. The
present situation is very acute and very difficult, but it ought not and I think will not be
beyond the power of the American government
and the American people to deal with it in a
spirit of justice that will both emphasize and
enforce our position as a neutral nation and
resist any effort to cloud the issue by irrelevant
appeals.

It is a fact that the way in which the neutrality of the United States has been mani-
fested in the present war has not wholly com-

mended us as a people to any one of the belligerent powers. This, perhaps, was to be expected, but it would be unfortunate if any feeling of criticism of the United States for having done some things and for having omitted to do others, should extend to the point of weakening European confidence in the ability and willingness of the American people to do justice between the belligerents and the policies they represent when this war shall come to an end, or in their capacity to grasp the real underlying issues of the war itself.

The notion that the present struggle is merely a European war, in which no one has any interest except the governments and citizens of the several belligerent powers is grotesque. It is a world war in which every neutral power is more or less involved, and the huge cost of which every neutral power will be called upon to share more or less heavily. It may be safely predicted that when the bills are all in and receipted a generation or two hence, the cost to the people of the United States will prove to have been stupendous. All these are reasons why the world power of the American democracy ought of right to be exerted and should, as a matter of policy and of national interest, be exerted when hostilities shall end, to compose the differences and the difficulties out of which this war has grown, and to remove their causes; and they are also reasons why nothing should be done which will weaken our world influence.

It is a very difficult and delicate matter to suggest to another people that one's own form of government is better than that which, at the moment, others enjoy. This is something which the United States could not formally or officially do. Nevertheless, it would be sheer hypocrisy to conceal the fact that the public opinion of the United States is substantially unanimous in holding that the peace of the world is more secure when foreign relations and foreign policies are determined and controlled by representatives of the people, than when these are wholly confided to dynasties or to diplomats, however beloved or however talented. The democratic principle cannot be said to insure international peace, but with equal certainty it can be said to make impossible certain kinds of war. It makes impossible all those numerous wars that grow out

of dynastic ambitions and policies, out of secret alliances and out of confidential understandings of one sort and another between
monarchs and foreign offices. The democratic
principle for which the United States stands
and which, after allowing for all mistakes and
inequities, it has done so much to advance,
diminishes the chance of conflict based upon
difference in religion and difference in race,
by insisting that neither of these differences
be given any recognition before the law. It is
obvious that if the United States is to achieve
and to exercise a world power based upon its
sincere democracy, we must have a care that
at home these principles are always kept clearly
in mind and are not departed from in our own
political practice. We have among us a good
many persons, and some groups of importance
and considerable size, that are not inclined to
be any too particular about insisting upon the
application of these fundamental democratic
principles, if, by overlooking them, they themselves can gain some immediate political or
personal end. To all such it may be pointed
out that while, of course, a nation must protect
itself, morally, intellectually, and physically,

yet it must protect itself by the application of its fundamental principles and not by the denial or forgetfulness of them.

One trait the people of the United States possess to an extent that never before has been recorded in the history of any nation, and that is the admirable trait of generosity and of sympathy for the distressed, the afflicted, and the stricken in any part of the world. Recognition of this fact must add greatly to our world influence. At the very time that some European observers have been denouncing the American people as mere traders, making money and gain out of the distressful conflict in Europe, those same American people have been pouring out not only millions of dollars, but life, energy, and service in the effort to carry food and clothing to the starving and ill-clad Belgians, to eliminate the fearful plague of typhus in Serbia, and to aid in giving the best medical and surgical service to the sick and wounded in the armies of Germany, Austria, Russia, France, and Great Britain. It may very well be doubted if anywhere in history there is recorded an equal display, prompt and overwhelming, of generous aid and tender human sympathy, regardless of the station, rank, nationality, or opinions of those who needed help. These facts reveal a people playing the Good Samaritan on a huge scale, and they illustrate what is meant by world leadership based on ideals. The nation whose people render services like these will never be forgotten in tens of thousands of villages and farm firesides all the way from the North Sea to the Caucasus.

If one is asked what power the United States can exert at the conclusion of this war, no definite answer can be given at the moment, because everything will depend upon which of the combatants is victorious. In any case, however, the United States ought to direct the attention of the nations now belligerent to these specific points:

First, that the various Hague Conventions, solemnly entered into in 1899 and in 1907, have been violated frequently since the outbreak of hostilities, and that, obviously, some greater and more secure sanction for such Conventions must be provided in the future.

Second, that in not a few instances the rules and usages of international law have been thrown to the winds, to the discredit of the belligerents themselves and to the grave distress, physically and commercially, of neutral powers.

Of course every one understands that international law is merely a series of conventions without other than moral sanction. If, however, the world has gone back to the point where a nation's plighted faith is not moral sanction enough, then that fact and its implications ought to be clearly understood and appropriate punitive action provided for.

Third, that any attempt to submerge nationalities in nations other than their own is certain to result in friction and conflict in the not distant future. Any attempt to create new nations, or to enlarge or diminish the area of nations, without having regard to nationality, is simply to organize a future war.

Fourth, that the transfer of sovereignty over any given district or people without their consent is certainly an unwise and probably an unjust action for any government to take, having regard for the peace and happiness of the world.

Fifth, that the international organization

which had been carried so far in such fields as maritime law, postal service, railway service, and international arbitration, should be taken up anew and pursued more vigorously, but upon a sounder and a broader foundation, and made a certain means of protecting the smaller and the weaker nations.

Sixth, that competitive armaments, instead of being an assurance against war, are a sure cause of war and an equally certain preventive of those policies of social reform and advance that enlightened peoples everywhere are eager to pursue.

Everything would depend upon the sincerity, the good temper, and the sympathy with which suggestions such as these were made and followed up. A first step toward the accomplishment of these ends is to create what some of us have long hoped for and felt to be possible, and what Mr. Asquith, in one of the greatest speeches made since the war began, clearly indicated to be within the range of practical statesmanship—namely, a method by which the nations of Europe may be so organized as to develop a common will. When that step is taken then the United States can point out the lessons which the history of our own federal system so clearly teaches.

No one in his senses could suppose that Europe, with its varied races and languages, could ever be welded into such a national unit as the United States, where a diverse population rests on a common English speech and the English common law; but the principle which the United States Government exemplifies is applicable, in my judgment, *mutatis mutandis*, to a United States of Europe. The beginnings of the central organ of the common will would probably be very simple and very slight. They might be chiefly judicial in character; if so, then so much the better. It will not be forgotten that some of the justices of the first United States Supreme Court wanted to resign because no case came before the Court for a year after it was organized. They said there was apparently no need for such a court and that there was nothing for it to do.

The world could very well afford to have Europe begin in the same simple way and trust to the force of ideas and the interest of nations in co-operation—their financial, their commercial, their intellectual interest—to strengthen

and to develop whatever organ they chose to
create at the outset.

The greatest achievements of the United
States have always tended toward peace, even
when they have been warlike. The Spanish
War was not an attack upon a people at peace,
but a war for the purpose of stopping war.
The events of the early spring and the summer
of 1898 are sometimes spoken of as the Span-
ish-American War. To me they have always
seemed more like the doing of such work as the
police and fire departments combined might be
called upon to perform in a great city. What
was done then by the United States was, to all
intents and purposes, to suppress a riot and to
put out a conflagration. If the United States
had enriched itself as a result of that action by
annexing the island of Cuba, the action itself
would have lost all its moral significance.

Through the action taken at the instance of
Senator Teller of Colorado and that taken at
the instance of Senator Platt of Connecticut—
although in fairness to both the living and the
dead it ought to be said that the strongest influence in drafting the Platt Amendment was
that of Elihu Root—the United States made it

plain that what it was doing was done in the interest of the people of Cuba and in the interest of humanity. In the large sense, therefore, this whole undertaking was a policy making for peace, for good order, for human happiness. In the same way it was to a President of the United States and to his Secretary of State that the governments of Japan and Russia turned, in the spring of 1905, with a view to securing assistance in bringing the costly and bloody conflict in Manchuria to an end. Both through its action in regard to Cuba and its action in regard to the Russo-Japanese War, to say nothing of its consistent attitude toward the government and the people of China, the United States has won the regard and the respect of thoughtful and liberal-minded men in all parts of the globe. It is such acts as these which promote world confidence in us and assure world power for us.

It is not possible to touch upon these topics without some mention of Mexico, where conditions are extremely difficult and very perplexing. There is no use now in discussing what might have been done three years ago or two years ago that would have led to an improve-

ment in the existing situation. The undisputed
facts are that chaos rules in Mexico, that
American lives have been sacrificed and others
are in danger, and that much property belong-
ing to Americans has been damaged or destroyed, and more of it is still threatened with
damage or destruction. Is it quite clear that
the people of the United States have no duty
whatever in regard to this matter, but should
merely stand aside and let the various armed
bands of Mexicans kill each other indefinitely,
as well as destroy the lives and property, not
only of Americans, but of citizens of European
nations? Are we or are we not our brothers'
keepers? These questions are not to be lightly
answered, for anything that would plunge us
into war with the Mexican people, or anything
that might possibly lead to an extension of our
territory or increase of our wealth at their expense, would be deplorable, and perhaps disastrous to us. Nor could we take any line of
action that would expose us to suspicion in the
minds of other American republics on the ground
that the United States, as an Anglo-Saxon and
Anglo-Celtic nation, was oppressing a Latin
people or aggrandizing itself at their expense.

The policy which most commends itself to my judgment, if a task similar to that performed seventeen years ago in Cuba ultimately becomes necessary, is to communicate our plans and policies to the governments of the other American republics and to ask the co-operation of at least some of them—for example, that of Argentina, Brazil, Chili, Uruguay, and Peru—in putting into effect whatever policies of a police character were jointly determined to be necessary in the interest of civilization and that of the Mexican people themselves. If it be objected that no one of these American republics has any direct interest in Mexico, the answer is that we have a very direct interest in having them have a sufficient interest in Mexico to protect us from misunderstanding and unfriendly criticism on their own part.

It is earnestly to be hoped that the Mexican people will speedily find some way of restoring orderly government for themselves, but it must be confessed that every week that passes makes the prospect of this seem less likely. Of course, it is not possible for a policeman or a fireman to attempt to settle a row in the street without running some risk of getting hurt, but that risk would be reduced to a minimum if the confidence and co-operation of a half-dozen other American republics were secured before the task was undertaken at all. Such an act would, of itself, be an illustration of what is meant by exercising world power. It would illustrate the value of bringing other free and enlightened peoples to our side to perform a public-spirited act, and it would illustrate and emphasize the moral purpose of performing that act in the interest of Mexico and the Mexican people without any thought or purpose of self-aggrandizement. It would give a new and generous interpretation to the Monroe Doctrine.

Our people have not yet appreciated how much we need, and would profit by, closer friendship and fuller understanding with the peoples of the other American republics. Every one of the efforts now being made to bring those peoples nearer to us, to understand more completely their point of view, their history, their literature, their institutions, and every effort to break down the barrier of language which separates us, deserve the heartiest support. The relation we seek with them is not a relation in which we are to exercise power, but one in which we and they together are to exercise an influence that is higher and better than mere power, because it is the outgrowth of our common devotion to democratic institutions and our complete and sympathetic understanding of what the very word America typifies and signifies.

There are other things which indicate a growth of such world power in the hands of the United States. Robert College at Constantinople on the banks of the Bosporus, and the American Protestant College at Beirut in Syria, are two of the most extraordinary examples of American influence anywhere in the world. Practically every leader of the liberal movement in Bulgaria has been educated in Robert College, which is supported entirely by American money, and the most enlightened young Turks, Arabs, and Greeks are to be found among the 400 or 500 students in the Syrian Protestant College at Beirut. These institutions represent the New England college transferred to the shores of the Mediterranean and to the banks of the Bosporus, and they are teaching, not only the usual letters, science, and philosophy, but American ideals, American

thought, American institutions to the young
men who are shaping or are going to shape the
civilization of the Eastern Mediterranean countries.

A great many of our European friends believe, as I myself believe, that a concomitant
and necessary element of international peace is
industrial peace, and there has recently been
sent to Europe all the information obtainable
regarding Mr. Henry Ford's profit-sharing undertaking at Detroit, and also that regarding
the United States Steel Corporation's capital
plan for caring for and helping its workers.
All this helps to build up world power for
the United States. This is what is meant by
the peaceful infiltration of ideas. It goes
much further than the work of the diploma-
tist; it works away down under the surface of
life.

Buy help + give a helping
and to other nations.
religion —
Schools etc ..
Mexico. —

V

PATRIOTISM

An Address delivered before the Newport Historical
Society, Newport, R. I., August 16, 1915

PATRIOTISM

A society like this—one of many score, many hundred, in this country and in other lands—is a very hearthstone of patriotism. It is by labors and by sacrifices such as yours that careful, affectionate, and accurate record is made of men and women, of happenings, of events, of undertakings, of movements of opinion and of action that are worth remembering. Your Society and other societies like-minded bring these records together, and make of them a hearthstone on which the fire of patriotism begins to burn; for the beginning of patriotism is love of home and all that home means, and through it comes the entering into the hopes and ideals and purposes of that larger home which constitutes our country.

Perhaps you have not all reflected upon what this thing called patriotism is and how recently it has come into the history of man. There was nothing corresponding to what we mean by patriotism in the older world. There was loyalty to race; there was something approaching patriotism, perhaps, in the life of the Greek or Roman city; there was loyalty to ruling monarchs or dynasties; there was pride of origin or opinion; but so long as the nations of Europe and America were in the making, so long as life was fluid, and men were moving uneasily and rapidly over the face of the earth, without fixed habitat or permanent institutions, there was nothing corresponding to what we know as patriotism. Nor is patriotism compatible with any ambition for world-empire or dominion. So long as there was hope of bringing the whole world under the dominion of a single form of religion or under the control of a single governing power—so long as those dreams flitted before the eyes and minds of men—there was nothing corresponding to what we know as patriotism.

Patriotism began to rise when the modern nations took on their form; when each group of men found itself in a separate and substantially fixed habitat; when unity of language began to develop; when literature sprang up on the wings of language; when institutions and achievements began to appear and to organize themselves; and when men began to convene and to feel the need of a social and political life that had an end or a purpose of its own which they could understand and teach to their children. When there was something that could be handed down, some theory of life, some theory of social relationship, some theory of the status which each man bears to his fellow, then there began to emerge the materials out of which patriotism is made.

But only a hundred and fifty years ago, more or less, the word had a very sinister and ugly meaning. I remember once reading in the letters of Horace Walpole the statement that the most helpful declaration that could be made upon the hustings in England, was that the speaker was not then and never had been a patriot. For in the seventeenth century and in the early part of the eighteenth, the word patriot was almost synonymous with disturber, with revolutionist—almost synonymous with anarchist, as we use the term so frequently, and often so incorrectly, to-day.

Later, particularly in connection with the beginning of the life of this nation, the words "patriot" and "patriotism" began to take on a healthier, a more sympathetic, and a finer

meaning, and those healthier, more sympathetic, and finer meanings have attached themselves to these words, until now the idea they
convey and represent is one to which we are
all glad to do honor.

A patriot is a man who stands to his country
in the relation of a father to his child. He
loves it; he cares for it; he makes sacrifices for
it; he fights for it; he serves it; he tries to shape
its course of thought and action, that it may
most perfectly adhere to its purpose and its
ideal.

We do not know—and no history, no science, no philosophy is yet wise enough fully
to instruct us—the significance and meaning of
each of the great civilizations of the modern
world; but despite the present desperate and
fearful clash of arms, we may be sure that
there is a place for each one of them—that each
serves some purpose, makes some contribution,
casts some reflection from the facet of its racial
nature and national organization. Some purpose is fulfilled by each one of them, and each
contributes its single beam, to help make the
full, white light of civilization. We may be
certain that to strike out from modern life any

one of the great national elements which enter into it would be to make it poorer, and would be to disarrange and to throw out of harmony the ever-moving plan of that civilization which has been built up by such hard and long work over so many centuries. Therefore we must have a care that we do not define patriotism as a cynic once defined it, as dislike of another country masked in the guise of love for our own.

There is no necessary conflict in the mind of the wise, well-instructed patriot, between the cause and purpose and aim of his nation and the cause and purpose and aim of the whole great group and family of nations. A patriot is not a termagant; he is not a destroyer of the peace; he is not one who treats with contempt or dislike his fellow who speaks another tongue or who owes allegiance to another flag or who loves another literature; but he is one who understands and appreciates how these various aspects of civilized life can better serve the common purpose by better serving each its own.

If a man or a woman is to rise to a true appreciation of patriotism and wishes to be a real patriot, then he or she must reflect upon the purpose of organized community life. I think it was Bishop Berkeley—whose name is so closely associated with this colony and this settlement—who said in substance that those who never reflect upon the great problems of the end and aim and purpose of life might be suitable to belong to a colony of industrious animals, but never could rise to the height of being men and women.

Instead of rhetoric, a patriot needs philosophy; instead of noisy and tumultuous expression of high feeling, he needs serious purpose, insight into the significance of his own country, a knowledge of its history, of its great personalities, of its policies, of its achievements, and above all, a knowledge of its aim. He must ask himself not only, "From what origin and by what steps has it come?" but more insistently and more emphatically, "Toward what end and toward what purpose is it moving? What is the reason of it all?"

We Americans are fortunate above all peoples, in that those searching questions have been answered for us in two great classic documents, written in language so simple that the mass of the people can read and understand them—documents which should be familiar, word by word, sentence by sentence, paragraph by paragraph, to every reflecting and educated American. I mean, of course, George Washington's Farewell Address, and the great Second Inaugural Address of Abraham Lincoln.

When George Washington was asked to permit his name to be used for the third time as candidate for the presidency, he declined in a noteworthy document, addressed to his fellow citizens. He not only set forth the reasons—the personal reasons—which actuated his declination of a third term as President, but he went further, and expounded and commended to his countrymen the principles of the country whose father he truly was. That document—one of the most precious in American history or American literature—should be a veritable guide-book for the American patriot. And then, nearly three-quarters of a century later, when the epoch-making civil struggle was nearing its end, the great heart of Abraham Lincoln poured itself out in words whose simple, compelling eloquence have rarely been equalled, when he for the second time ascended the steps of the Capitol to take the oath of office as President of the United States. He, too, from another point of view, but in no less practical ways and with no less generous purpose, pressed home upon his countrymen the principles to which their loyalty was due.

The American patriot will inform himself upon those two great documents. He will like to read them, to quote them, to think upon them, to turn to them and to their principles, to seek their instruction in determining his own position in regard to the thousand and one practical questions of the moment, which are simply the old questions of human ambition, human greed, and human folly, dressing themselves up in new forms, and joining the never-ending procession of progress toward human excellence, that goes to make up human history.

The Farewell Address of Washington, and the Second Inaugural of Lincoln, are for the American a corner-stone upon which to build a sure and abiding structure of true patriotism.

Our country is unique, not as we so often think and say because of its size, not because of its population, not because of its wealth, not because of its variety of products and climates, not because of its temperaments and racial elements—though they all enter into its greatness, and will form subjects for the future historian to analyze and interpret—but it is unique in that we have managed for now more than a century and a quarter, to build into permanence principles of government and of life which had been the ideal of dreamers for more than a thousand years. Very few of those dreamers ever supposed that in the nineteenth and twentieth centuries there would arise on this earth a great nation, built upon those principles, dedicated to them, and successfully exemplifying their operation and practice over this amazing extent of territory. No one would have supposed this to be possible.

We need not stop to dwell upon our shortcomings; we need not stop to analyze and to explain our feelings of difficulty and of doubt or to make lists of the things we should like to do, but have not done. All that is known and admitted by us, by our friends, and by our critics; but at a moment like this, when the whole world appears to be in a state of flux, when all old standards seem to be thrown to the winds, it is worth while to dwell upon the permanent and progressive forward movement in American life, and to take account and make measure of its achievements and its triumphs.

This country is, in a peculiar sense, the keeper of the conscience of democracy. There may be nations—we know there are nations of the first rank—not committed as we are to the democratic principle. We need find no fault with them for preferring, temporarily at least, some other form of social and political organization; but we must bear in mind that we are the keepers of the democratic conscience of the world. We are the keepers of the open door of opportunity in democracy; and we are the keepers of the great principle of federation as a means of securing domestic freedom and national unity, and of permitting liberty under law in ways with which we have now been familiar for nearly a century and a half.

The greatest problem of men in all history has been the question how to secure both government and liberty. How to preserve order without suppression of the individual, how to promote the common good without depriving the individual of initiative, how to weld men into a mass, into a new and higher order, without destroying personal identity—that problem in its most serious sense is ours.

The true American patriot will never permit himself to lose sight of the fact that the line between government and liberty is the line upon which he must keep his eye, and the line toward which he must hew, let the chips fall where they will.

If all individual initiative be transferred to the realm of government, we have no opportunity for that individual life which has been the glory of our modern world. If we transfer all the fundamental elements of a well-ordered government over to the realm of liberty, we have national dissolution and political death. The American patriot, keeping his heart open and his mind free from prejudice, seeking friendships everywhere in this world and enmities nowhere, keeping his eye fixed on this line between government and liberty, will ask himself how, as one of the keepers of the democratic conscience, can he act in a given crisis, in the presence of a given problem, before a given issue—how can he act, my friends, so as to protect the aim and the ideals of the American Republic?

He is a poor American who is without a passionate love of home; who does not feel a peculiar drawing at the heart and a choking of the voice when his mind goes back in after-years to the home where his first associations were made, where his father and mother lived, where his childhood friends and associates, his school-teachers and schoolmates dwelt, where he got his first outlook on life and began to stretch his wings and try to fly. No temporary abiding-place, no working-place or office or house can ever be substituted for the home in the heart of the true patriot. Just so the patriot's feeling for his fatherland or motherland is the feeling he has for the nation to which he belongs, the ideal to which he owes allegiance, the language he speaks, the literature he loves, and the law that determines the patriot's relation to all of these—his intelligence, reflections, and emotions—the relation of the individual to his larger home.

It is out of the home that the nation is built. It is out of the home's purposes and ideals that the nation gains aim and substance, and it is in the home that the controlling moral and intellectual principles that shape government and organization take form and gain their truest significance. There is no subject fuller of meaning than this age-old subject of a man's relation to his fathers. Now that we have learned in these modern days to cast it into the form of this patriotism which I am trying briefly to describe, now that we have learned to see it in the moral and intellectual and religious relation, we can look forward to the day when we shall learn to see in it no place for enmity, national or international. We may justly hope to look out upon that future day, when the patriots of every nation will find their greatest satisfaction in co-operating and combining toward the perfection of the great humanitarian ideal throughout the world.

We dare not close our eyes in pessimism because to-day we hear the thunder of guns and the cries of the wounded and the dying. Terrible as that is, terrible as the reason for it is, I beg you to believe that it is only an episode—a dismal, tragic episode, but an episode—in the forward march of an idea and a purpose which no armaments can permanently check. This is not a purposeless world. This is not a ball, plunging through space, with no orbit, subject to no law of control, existing as part of no system, serving no purpose. The physicist tells us that if we disturb in the very slightest degree any physical element in the universe, we affect its remotest circumference. What of the human elements? What of the importance and the balance which they have, the ideas, the feelings, and the acts of will which are the embodiments of ideas, that are carried forward into the making of institutions? Those are the great things in history. We see them spring into life and enter one nation after another.

There is a place for the Oriental; there is a place for the Occidental; there is a place for the European; there is a place for the American; just as there is a place in the great stout strand that binds the ship to the boat that tows it, for every one of the little threads that wound together make it what it is. Take that great strand apart and a child could snap each thread. Wind them tight together so that every one supports the other, and it would take a superman to tear that rope apart.

This problem of institution building—whether

by the people of one nation or by the peoples of all nations of the world together—is the one that will be supremely important when the curtain falls upon the tragedy that now moves its slow course to the pain and distress and grief of every patriot in every land.

VI

THE CHANGED OUTLOOK

An Address delivered at the One Hundred and Forty-
Seventh Annual Banquet of the Chamber of
Commerce of the State of New York,
November 18, 1915

THE CHANGED OUTLOOK

Four years ago I had the privilege of speaking in this presence. At that time I chose as my subject, "Business and Politics." We were then approaching the end of a presidential term and facing a national election; we were concerned, gravely concerned, with domestic problems, particularly with those manifold and important questions which arise out of the relations between government and business. To-night I have chosen as the topic on which to speak to you, quite informally and briefly, "The Changed Outlook"; for in the interval of those four years there has been a revolution in our thinking and a complete change in the prospect that opens out before us. Once again we are approaching the end of a presidential term and once again we are facing a national election, but the outlook to-day is strangely and solemnly different from what it was four years ago.

It is not easy for one who lives in the midst of onrushing events to judge calmly and accu-

rately either of their significance or of their
direction. The man who is borne helplessly
down-stream by a roaring torrent has little
opportunity to observe the foliage that may
adorn the banks, or to determine with certainty
whether he is to be dashed to pieces by the
cataract of Niagara or borne harmlessly into
the peaceful waters of a mountain lake. So it
is with ourselves. The wild onrush of events
in a world at war; the sudden and startling
changes in finance, in commerce, in industry;
the quick movement of armies and of navies
by which some of the hopes and ambitions of
two generations are gratified; the dazed per-
plexity of the world's most trusted leaders—
all these are characteristic of the days through
which we are living.

When the midsummer sun set on the eve-
ning of Friday, July 31, 1914, it set upon a
world upon which it was never to rise again.
Never again was that sun to rise upon the
same world. As if by magic, transportation
and communication stopped; the wells of credit
were dried up; commerce and industry were
brought to a standstill; men leaped to arms
and to the assembling of the devilishly in-

genious instruments of destruction; science which had been caring for the health, the comfort, and the prosperity of man was instantly bent with amazing ingenuity and skill to the wholesale slaughter of human beings and to the destruction and waste of property on a scale unprecedented in all recorded history. This is neither the time nor the place to inquire why these strange and startling things took place. It is sufficient to observe that they did take place and that the whole world order was changed in a night.

The peoples who are engaged in this titanic struggle are not untamed barbarians or wild Indians of the virgin forest. They are the best-trained and most highly educated peoples in the world. They have had every advantage that schools and universities can offer, and they have been associated for generations with literature and science and art and everything that is fine and splendid in what we call civilization. What we now know, even those of us who were most loath to believe it, is that under this thin veneer of civilization the elementary human passions of jealousy, envy, hatred, and malice were so lightly confined that at the

touch of a magic spring they burst forth to
overwhelm everything that seems to make life
worth living. Moreover, it is now so plain
that even the dullest can see that the nations
of Europe had been psychologically, politically,
and even strategetically, at war for many years.
In the guise of an armed peace they were really
in conflict, and jealousy, suspicion, and in-
trigue were abroad on every hand. Plans of
instant mobilization and of quick attack were
all in readiness, and the more ardent spirits
were tugging hard at the bonds of convention-
ality that restrained them from overt acts.
Europe had been at war for years. What happened on August 1, 1914, was that the curtain was lifted so that all men might see; and
the physical conflict of armies and navies followed as a final and dramatic incident in a
contest which was on that day made evident,
but which was not on that day begun.

If I read history aright, only once before since
the beginning of man's records has any similar
catastrophe occurred in the Western world.
With the downfall of the Roman Empire and
the inrush of the barbarian hordes from the
forests and plains of the North there was a

wiping out of Greek and Roman civilization and of their evidences that was as complete as it was terrible. From that day to this there has been no similar cataclysm in Europe. There have been wars, many and severe. There have been revolutions devastating and terrible. There has been the spectacle of the great Napoleon defying the whole of Europe, but finally succumbing to the power of his adversaries. But not since the break-up of Roman civilization has the world seen anything that can compare with what is now going on before our eyes. Europe, Asia, Africa, and Australia are being tramped by contending armies or are held in the grip of the laws of war.

It is idle to say, quite idle to say, that the American people are on the other side of the world and that these clashings and crashings are no concern of theirs. Ask the cotton grower in the South, or the copper miner in the far West, or the lumberman on Puget Sound, or the shipper in New York, in Baltimore, or New Orleans, or the banker in Wall Street, in State Street, or in La Salle Street, whether he knows that there is a war in Europe, and get his answer. Ask the student of international law, or the expounder of political ethics and the sanctity of treaties, or the devoted believer in civil liberty, whether the United States has any interest in this conflict, and get his answer!

It is no longer possible for the United States, ostrich-like, to plunge its head into the sands of a supposed isolation and to assume that its policies, its influences, and its ideals are not part of the wider world. The outlook has wholly changed. The future, and in particular the immediate future, is charged with serious international interest and with heavy international responsibility. Of this interest we cannot divest ourselves, and of this responsibility we dare not, without proving false to our trust as keepers of the faith in civil liberty as the highest political aim and object of mankind.

There are reasons, good and sufficient and easily understood by the reader of history, why America's interest in international conditions is now much greater and much more important than ever before. In the history of peoples, it is a well-known fact that internal national development must precede international influence and direction. Not until a nation has unified itself, perfected reasonably well its instruments of government and become conscious of an ideal and of a mission which that ideal serves, can it be ready to take its place at the council table of nations and to exercise a shaping influence in the formulation and carrying out of world policies. That time has now come in the history of the United States. We have expanded across the continent, and have settled and developed the waste places. We have established, after a long debate, and by an epoch-making military struggle, the unity of the nation and the supremacy of the national ideal. We have developed great systems of transportation and manifold industries, and we have accumulated vast national wealth. We have made creditable contributions to science, to literature, and to the arts. The question now to press upon ourselves is, Are we ready and equipped to bear the responsibilities that the close of this war will place upon the American people? Are we prepared?

In one of the noblest orations of antiquity Pericles used these words in speaking to his fellow citizens of the Athenians who had died in the war with Sparta: "The whole earth is the sepulchre of famous men; and their glory is not graven only on stone over their native earth, but lives on far away, without visible symbol, woven into the stuff of other men's lives. For you it now remains to rival what they have done, and, knowing the secret of happiness to be freedom and the secret of freedom to be a brave heart, squarely to face the war and all its perils." Surely these sonorous words sounding across the centuries seem almost to have been meant for our ears to hear. We are to weave our lives, our aspirations, and our ideals into the stuff of other men's lives; we are to remember that the secret of happiness is freedom and that the secret of freedom is a brave heart, and then we are squarely to face this war and all that it brings in its train.

There is much earnest speech among us in regard to national preparedness, and it is urged by many and influential voices that we must beware lest the calamity that fell so suddenly upon Europe should be forced against our wish or will upon us. Surely we must reckon with facts as they are, and not as we would wish them to be. We may turn our faces to the stars, but we must have a care to keep our feet on the firm ground. Nevertheless, there is a more serious and a more important aspect of national preparedness that has not yet been so much dwelt upon. Our chiefest task is to prepare our hearts and our minds to do our full duty as Americans to bind up the wounds of a stricken world and to lead the way to that new construction of the overturned political fabric which, if it is to endure, can rest upon no other principles than those of democracy, of freedom, of civil liberty, of international responsibility and honor, to which we profess such earnest allegiance and through faith in which our nation has grown great.

It is true of nations, as of men, that we are our brothers' keepers. Their interests are increasingly our interests, and our interests are increasingly theirs. We have no wish or will to interfere with problems that belong to Europe alone; but surely non-interference does not mean absence of interest in them or an absence of influence upon them or over them. In the Monroe Doctrine, in the policy of the Open Door, and in the wide-spread objection to Oriental immigration, we have given concrete evidences of a developed and developing international view-point and international policy. We must, by taking counsel together, by study and by reflection, prepare ourselves to say to a listening world what our international policy is and what it is to be; what influence we aim to exert and why, and what ideals we propose to hold aloft in the hope that they may guide and help other peoples.

Before we can hope to influence others we must be sure of ourselves. We must without delay undertake the better conservation and organization of our own national resources of every kind. We must make it plain that, by voluntary effort and without sacrificing our traditional American principles to the demands of a bureaucratic organization, we too can effectively mobilize the industrial resources of a great nation. It is for American democracy to prove that it can secure the highest type of national preparedness and the highest type of national effectiveness without ceasing to be either American or democratic. In the recently established Trade Commission and in the Tariff Commission, whose quick establishment is so strongly supported, we shall have governmental instrumentalities which might readily be made the centre for co-operative industrial effort and for the more complete equipment of this nation in respect to all the great basic industries. The problem of labor must be faced with courage, with frankness, and with sympathy; for industrial peace and satisfaction is as necessary a prerequisite of international peace and contentment as it is of national security and happiness.

Moreover, it behooves us to cultivate a becoming national modesty. It was Mr. Bryce who pointed out to us in the *American Commonwealth* that the enormous force of public opinion is a danger, a danger to the people themselves as well as to their leaders, because it fills them with an undue confidence in their own wisdom, their own virtue, and their own freedom. In order to guard ourselves against the vice of self-complacency we must constantly re-examine and restate our moral and our political ideals, and we must not fail to give due weight to the moral and political ideals of other people.

The world mission that we might have waited for through another century has come to us to-day from the hand of fate. We can remain true to the injunction of Washington that we steer clear of permanent alliances with any portion of the foreign world, and yet do our full international duty; for what we should seek is not an alliance, entangling or otherwise, with any portion of the foreign world, but rather relations with the whole of that world and with every part of it, in order that in a spirit of friendship and good temper and constructive statesmanship we may do our full share in raising that world to a higher plane.

No one dares predict just what the end of this world war will be or when that end will come. It is possible, of course, that this cataclysm marks the end of centuries of progress, and it is possible that man in 1914 crossed over the watershed of civilization and is now to descend on the other side toward steadily growing barbarism and the steadily extending rule of force. That I say is possible; but I for one am an unconquerable optimist. I prefer to read history differently and to see in this appalling catastrophe what the Greek called a *katharsis*, or cleansing of the spirit. I prefer to think of it as history's way of teaching beyond peradventure or dispute the fallacy and the folly of the old ways and the old policies. Surely that struggle for the balance of power which the historian Stubbs described as the principle which gives unity to the plot of modern history—surely that struggle has proved its futility. Surely we can see the vanity of Ententes and Alliances and of a division of the world into heavily armed camps, each waiting for an opportunity or for an excuse to pounce upon the other.

A democratic federated people can teach the world democracy and the use of the federative principle. A people devoted to civil liberty and to international honor, no less lightly held than the honor of an individual—that people can teach the world the foundations upon which to rebuild the shattered fabric of international law and of broken treaties.

The outlook before the people of the United States has changed. When Joseph Chamberlain returned from South Africa his message to the people of Great Britain was: "You must learn to think imperially." The message which any American alive to the world's situation to-day must bring to his fellow citizens is, you must learn to think internationally! Domestic policies and problems are perhaps no less important than they have been in the past, but by their side and for the immediate future surpassing them in interest and in importance are the international problems and the international policies of the people of the United States. For those problems and for those policies we must prepare—prepare thoughtfully, seriously, speedily; for when the war shall be ended, we may truly say, as Gambetta said to the French people forty-five years ago: "Now that the danger is past, the difficulties begin."

The world need is conscious of fellowmen. The economic social & political conditions in full after war. To meet care yet the one must face prob. squarely + with that attempt to give solu for them.

VII

HIGHER PREPAREDNESS

An Address delivered before the Union League of
Philadelphia, November 27, 1915

HIGHER PREPAREDNESS

It was my lot to be born after the Civil War had begun and for me the name, the face, and the repute of Abraham Lincoln belong not to memory but to imagination. Yet I was brought up under the very shadow of his name, of his fame, and of his work. The events and circumstances of his life were among the earliest lessons that it was my fortune to learn. It seemed to me then, and it seems to me now, that Abraham Lincoln left to every American born after him a legacy in the form of a direct injunction to love his country, to study its needs, to make himself familiar with its policies and its problems, and to labor with those like-minded with himself for the advancement of all of these.

The era of Lincoln, of the Civil War, and of nation-building—that great classic era in the history of the western world and of all mankind —is closed. The problems that confronted the founders and the builders of our nation are still our problems, but they are presented to us in a different form. We are no longer a young people, but a comparatively old and well-established one. We are, thank God, a united people. We have solved, let us hope forever and finally, the problem of building a single great nation out of a group of federated States with diverse populations, with conflicting economic needs and desires, and we have opened our arms to the whole wide world that it may enter in and share with us and with our children the shelter and the protection of this noble structure. When so much has been done we find ourselves confronted with the problems of an older people and of a better-established civilization. It is no longer necessary for us to find men of energy and ambition to explore a continent, to bridge rivers, to fell forests, or to build railways across the desert; those are the problems of a new people, and we solved those problems in the generation that followed 1850 and 1860. Then came the problems incident to a more concentrated political and economic life—the problems of capital and labor, the problems of the growth of great corporate wealth, of the organization of business and of the development of public utilities, as well as

the relation of all these to government, both
State and national. During all this second
period, which was shorter than the first, very
intense and tremendously important, abounding in problems that touched the interests and
convictions of every citizen, we were still a self-
centred people. We had foreign relations, but
they were of minor importance. They occupied
the attention of the President, of the Depart-
ment of State, and of the Senate, but beyond
that they hardly existed for the great mass of
our American population. But now, in a
twinkling of an eye, the outlook that confronts
America has changed and we are about to
enter, perhaps it would be correct to say we
have already entered, upon a new and third
period of our political development and of our
intellectual and moral preoccupation. We are
now confronted with the fact, borne in upon
us in a thousand ways, that steam, electricity,
the use of the air, the development of modern
industry and finance, have conspired to destroy
distance and to eliminate time, and that these
have bound the whole world together in a new
and hitherto unsuspected sort of interdependence. Out of that interdependence of the

nations an interdependence of our nation with other nations of the world, comes the new series of problems for the consideration and the solution of which this nation must insistently and thoughtfully prepare.

The old world order changed when this war-storm broke. The old international order passed away as suddenly, as unexpectedly, and as completely as if it had been wiped out by a gigantic flood, by a great tempest, or by a volcanic eruption. The old world order died with the setting of that day's sun and a new world order is being born while I speak, with birth-pangs so terrible that it seems almost incredible that life could come out of such fearful suffering and such overwhelming sorrow.

What has America to do with it all? All these terrible clashings and crashings are on the other side of the world, from which we are separated by a great ocean. How do these matters affect us, secure in our protection across three thousand miles of sea, living under other political institutions and under the dominance of other political ideas and with different economic and social interests? To make answer to these questions our hearts guide our heads. We first feel, and then we see, the community of our interest with those peoples in Europe who are struggling against aggression for the maintenance of their own national life, their own undisturbed territory, and their own free institutions. The world cannot be cut in two any longer by an ocean or a mountain range. The several peoples of the earth are fellows and comrades and they cannot, if they would, isolate themselves completely from each other.

In this new outlook that confronts us we are not called upon, as I see it, to depart in principle or in practice from sound American policy, but we are called upon to consider whether new occasions do not teach new duties and whether new problems do not bring new opportunities and new obligations. I would not have the people of these United States forget the injunction of Washington. I would not have them depart from the path of established policy that has been trodden so long and on the whole so wisely. I would not have them make an alliance, entangling or otherwise, with any single nation or any group of nations on the globe. But I would have them enter into such relations of intimacy and influence with every nation that the spirit and convictions which animate and permeate the American people might be made a contribution to the world's civilization when this war ends. I would endeavor to show to Europe how here across the sea we have solved and are solving some problems that are in kind their problems. I would try to show to Europe that whatever may be the difficulties and the conflicts which grow out of differences of race and of creed and of language, those difficulties are only increased by political repression, while they are decreased by an extension of civil and political liberty. I would try to show that on the whole, and despite the dangers and difficulties and the many and obvious embarrassments which accompany it, a national policy of freedom, of hospitality, and of equal opportunity solves more problems than it leaves unsolved, and that on the whole it solves more political problems than any other alternative policy that has yet been presented for the government of men. I would not interfere for a moment with the internal concerns of any European nation or with their just ambitions, their alliances, and their rivalries, but at a time like this I would not throw away the lesson of a hundred and twenty-five years of life and government under the Constitution of the United States. I would make a world figure of Washington. I would make world figures of Hamilton and Jefferson, of Marshall and Webster. I would make a world figure of Abraham Lincoln. I would make their names, their faces, their public acts, and the great tendencies and institutions that they organized and represented the property of the whole civilized world for the benefit of all mankind. For this or for any such policy of international influence this nation must prepare.

We have been speaking much of late of preparedness, and properly so; but there is an aspect of this important question that has hardly been touched upon, and as to which the public mind is as yet almost completely uninformed. That question is this: What is to be the object of your preparedness? What are to be the policies that you are going to teach, to defend, and to extend over the earth? What are to be the ideals that you are going to hold up before yourselves and then before the other nations of the earth? Armies and navies are not ends; they are means. But means to what end? For what are we going to prepare? Are we going to prepare to make this nation first a model nation at home and then a model nation abroad? If we are going to do this, then we have a policy. If we are not going to do this, then we have no policy but only a proposal for expenditure.

Our American ideals are not vague or uncertain. They have been stated for us in language that the whole world can read, in words that will remain forever familiar where the history of freedom is read and studied. They have been written for us particularly in four great historic documents. You will find them in the opening paragraphs of the Declaration of Independence. You will find them in the preamble to the Constitution of the United States. You will find them in Washington's farewell address to the American people. You will find them put with all the terseness of classic literature in the immortal address of Abraham Lincoln on the battle-field of Gettysburg. Those great documents have stated for us the aims, the ideals, and the purposes of this government, as well as the aims, the ideals, and the purposes of the people in founding and in maintaining this government. It is for a fuller comprehension of those aims, those ideals, and those purposes, for a more complete carrying out of them at home, and for a more effective teaching of them abroad that we must prepare. We must prepare under the leadership of those who by experience, by training, by discipline, and by conviction are able to help us set our feet in these new paths. For it is as true to-day as it was when the prophet first said it, that where there is no vision the people perish.

The time has come when the American people must learn to think internationally. We must learn to think in terms of our relations with the whole world, and we must learn to think of other peoples than ourselves with such sympathy, with such kindliness, and with such understanding as will enable us to appreciate the point of view, the opinions, and the institutions of those whose experiences have been different from our own. I like to think that the hand of fate has brought to us out of this terrible war a new and unexpected call to achievement; first at home in putting our own house in order, and next abroad in teaching the peoples of the world a lesson that the founders and the fathers have taught us. In all this, however, we must walk circumspectly and without either pride or arrogance. We ourselves have still too much to learn to justify us in attempting the task of imposing, single-handed, new ideals upon the world. We can, however, and we should participate, with the open-minded and broad-minded of every land in the perpetual and persistent re-examination of our own principles, our own aims, our own purposes, and by conferring and consulting together as to how best we can advance this nation and every nation in paths of justice and of liberty.

We have great economic problems that are in part internal and that are in part international. There are signs that this new international era of which I speak is going to help us to solve some of our internal economic problems.

We have got to face under these new conditions the world-old problem of how to provide justly for equal opportunity, and how to provide an economic basis for individual existence in order that men may be able to live at all. It is hardly worth while to preach ideals of government to a starving man. We must provide, first, wisely, justly, and securely for our internal economic organization, in order that we may be able to do these new international deeds of which I speak. In other words, while our whole problem, national and international, is bound up together, it becomes immensely larger and immensely more important than it has ever been before, because we have now discovered these innumerable points of contact with other nations and we see the meaning and significance on one side of the world of some public act or economic policy that has its origin on the other. This is all a part of the task that I call learning to think internationally. It will affect our domestic problems and our domestic policies, as well as our foreign problems and our foreign policies.

Unless I mistake the signs of the times, this nation is crying out for leadership. It is crying out for a voice that will give expression to its political conviction and to its moral purpose in tones that every American will understand. Unless I mistake the signs of the times, the American people would like a leadership whose ear is not continually fastened to the ground.

We wish, we need, we long for a determined, clear, and sympathetic voice that will do for our day and generation what Abraham Lincoln did for his. A voice that will look down into the hearts of the plain people, that will know the conditions that influence their lives, that will understand the motives that guide their action, that will sympathize with their ambitions, with their difficulties, and with their failures, and that will call them up to the high places of the earth as did those voices that called our fathers up to their great achievement. Give us leadership. Give us a mind to seek, a heart to feel, and a voice to proclaim what the American people of this day and this generation aspire to do at home and abroad.

The main idea = leadership in this

VIII

THE BUILDING OF THE NATION

An Address delivered at the Annual Luncheon of the
Associated Press at the Waldorf-Astoria, New York,
April 25, 1916

THE BUILDING OF THE NATION

If any significance be attached to what I shall briefly say in your presence, it can only be because it represents the attempt of one American who feels keenly the responsibility of his country and of its entire citizenship at this moment when the world stands at a crossroads in its path of progress. If we stand at that crossroads irresolute, paralyzed of word and will, history will have one story to tell. If we turn to the right and take the path that leads upward to new achievement and to lasting honor, it will have a very different story to tell. If we should turn to the left and follow the winding and rocky road that leads down to a darkening gloom—we know not where—history will have yet another record to make of the American people and of their capacity to represent civilization.

It is just about twenty years ago since George Meredith, writing to the London *Daily News*, said that since the benignant outcome of the greatest of civil wars he had come to look upon the American people as the leaders in civilization. That is a proud and ennobling judgment, and we may well search our minds and our hearts to ascertain whether it be true, and whether we are competent for the high honor that so distinguished an observer of his kind proffered to us as his personal judgment.

The question which I ask in your presence this afternoon is this: Have we an American nation? If so, is that nation conscious of a unity of purpose and of ideals? If so, what is to be the policy of that nation in the immediate future?

Familiar as nations seem to us, they have not always existed in their present form. The new consciousness of unity that makes a nation is in part the outgrowth of unity of race origin, in part the outgrowth of unity of language, in part the outgrowth of unity of institutional life, in part the outgrowth of unity of military and religious tradition. It seized hold of the minds of men in most practical fashion. The result is that from the time of the death of Charlemagne to the time of the present German Emperor the history of the world is the history of nation-building and of the by-products of nation-building. Nation-building has proceeded usually by seeking out natural boundaries in order to gain the protection of lofty mountains, or of broad rivers, or of the sea itself. One war after another is to be explained in terms of a nation's definite purpose to possess itself of a geographic unity as its home. There has been by no means equal care taken by the nations to establish and to protect an ethnic unity. A strong people has usually felt confident that it could hold an alien element in subjection and yet preserve national integrity and unity of spirit. So one after another of the greater nations of the world has, in seeking for geographic unity, insisted on incorporating in its own body politic alien and often discordant elements and holding them in stern subjection. The examples are too familiar to be recited here.

This process of nation-building has gone on until the nation has come to be conceived as an end in itself, as superior to law, to the conventions of morality, and to the precepts of religion. A form of patriotism has been developed all over the world which finds in the nation itself the highest human end. The logical result, and indeed the almost necessary result, of this type of thinking is the war which is now creeping over the world's civilization and destroying it with the sure pitilessness of an Alpine glacier.

This war is the nemesis of nation-building conceived as an end in itself. Unless a nation, like an individual, have some purpose, some ideal, some motive which lies outside of and beyond self-interest and self-aggrandizement, war must continue on the face of this earth until the day when the last and strongest man, superb in his mighty loneliness, shall look out from a rock in the Caribbean upon a world that has been depopulated in its pursuit of a false ideal, and be left to die alone with none to mourn or to bury him.

In the history of nations the story of our America has a place that is all its own. The American nation came into being in response to a clear and definite purpose. A theory of human life and of human government was conceived and put into execution on a remote and inaccessible part of the earth's surface. The moving cause of the American nation was the aspiration for civil and political liberty and for

individual freedom which was already stirring
in the minds of western Europe in the sixteenth
and seventeenth centuries. This aspiration
gained in force as the art of printing multiplied
books, and as the periodical press came into
existence. The high-minded, the courageous,
the venturesome were drawn across the wide
ocean toward the west, carrying with them for
the most part the liberal ideas and the advanced
thought that were steadily increasing their
hold upon the people of western Europe. Great
Britain, Holland, France, were responding in
steadily increasing measure to the same ideals
that led the Puritan to Massachusetts Bay and
the Cavalier to Virginia.

On this Atlantic shore distances were great
and communication difficult. In addition there
were social, economic, and religious differences
that kept the struggling colonists apart. The
result was that there grew up here not a nation, but the material out of which a nation
could be made. There is a sense, a deep and
striking sense, in which the same remains absolutely true to-day. There is not yet a nation,
but the rich and fine materials out of which a
true nation can be made by the architect with

vision to plan and by the builder with skill adequate to execute.

When a common oppression forced the separate colonists together they still sadly lacked that devotion to a unity higher than any of its component parts which would have saved so much loss and so much suffering during the days of revolution and of the first steps toward a National Government. An enormous step forward was taken when the National Government was built. In the adoption of the Constitution of the United States, the corner-stone was laid for one of the most splendid structures in all the history of nations. Then quickly followed sharp political divergence. There were those who would lay stress upon the new national unity; there were still more who thought it important to emphasize the separate elements out of which that unity had been composed. The judicial logic of Marshall and the convincing eloquence of Webster were the chief unifying and nation-building forces in the generation that followed. Meanwhile sharp differences of economic interest were manifesting themselves, and the fatal question of slavery pressed forward both as an economic and as a political issue. The new nation, which had already made such progress upon the foundations laid by the fathers, fell apart, and only after one of the most terrible and destructive of civil wars were the ruins of the disaster cleared away and the ground prepared for the next step in construction. Here again mistakes were made so numerous and so severe that the unifying and nation-building process was checked and held back for many years.

Then two new sets of separating and disintegrating forces began to make themselves strongly felt. First, the economic differences which must of necessity manifest themselves over so large and so diverse a territory now revealed themselves with new force—in part as a result of the industrial revolution and in part as a result of purely American conditions—as involving a class conflict between capital and labor. Soon there were signs that citizenship, with its compelling allegiance to the common weal, was to be subordinated in discouraging fashion, not once but often, to the immediate interests and policies of an economic class.

Second, the immigration from other countries, which had been for a long time substantially homogeneous became increasingly and rapidly heterogeneous. New nationalities, new languages, new racial affinities were drawn upon for the recruitment of the population of the United States. The hopes and the ambitions which one hundred and two hundred years before had been the peculiar property of the people of Western Europe had now spread far away to the East and to the South. With this heterogeneous immigration there came, in no inconsiderable measure, the echo of the Old World animosities and feuds and hates. These did not manifest themselves in any direct sense as anti-American, but they did manifest themselves with sufficient strength to deprive America of a unity of attitude, of feeling, and of policy in dealing with the international relations which every day grow in importance and in significance.

So it is that at this moment, with a world war raging about us, with years full of fate stretched out for us to walk in, we are not sure of our national unity of thought and feeling and purpose because of the presence of disintegrating elements and forces which weaken our sense of unity at home and which deprive us of the influence abroad which attaches to unity at home. The grave problem before the American people to-day is that of completing the process of nation-building. It is the problem of setting our house in order. It is the problem of integrating America. It is the problem of subordinating every personal ambition, every class interest and policy, every race attachment, to the one dominant idea of an America free, just, powerful, forward-facing, that shall stand out in the history of nations as the name of a people who conceive their mission and their true greatness to lie in service to mankind. We are the inheritors of a great tradition. What poets and philosophers have dreamed, that we are trying day by day to do. Our stumblings, our blunders, our shortcomings are many; but if we keep our hearts clean and our heads clear he who a thousand years from now writes the history of liberty and justice and happiness among men will be able to tell to those far-off generations a proud story of the rise and influence of the American nation.

We find here everything which is needed for a great nation. The task before us to-day is to make it. The task before the American people is nothing more or less than a speedy continuation, and, if it be practicable, the completion of the process of nation-building. It is the problem of the integration of America about those great fundamental principles and purposes which the very name America itself brings to our minds and which this flag stirs to expression on every lip.

We know in our heart what America means. The problem is to teach it to our fellows; to share with them an understanding and an appreciation of it; to unite with them in an expression of it. We wish to build a nation fit to serve; a nation that does not find its end in its own aggrandizement, however great that be; a nation that cannot find its purpose complete in amassing all the wealth of Golconda, but that can only achieve its aim by carrying a message to mankind of what has been found possible on this continent. Saxon and Celt, Teuton and Slav, Latin and Hun, all are here not as aliens but as citizens; not as immigrants but as members of a body politic which is new in conception in human history, as it is new in its own thought of its high purpose. Can America integrate itself at this crisis; can it show that here is a nation which, out of various and varied ethnic elements, can be brought into a genuine unity by devotion to high principle and by moral purpose before the face of all mankind? Can we make an America that shall go down the corridors of time with a proud place on the pages of history?

We must remember that the greatest empires have fallen as well as risen. We must remember that the most powerful dynasties have passed away as well as come into existence. There is no reason to suppose that our America is going to escape the everlasting law of change. We know its history and its origin. We have seen its rise. We know its present state. Who can predict how many hundreds or thousands of years it will take before the forests will be felled and the streams will be dried, and this great fertile continent of ours, like the plains of ancient Iran, where civilization began, will become a desert, fit only for the exploring parties of the archæologist? When that time comes, what do we want to have written on the pages of history of those who lived for hundreds or perhaps thousands of years on this continent? What do we want to have said about the way in which America met the greatest crisis of the world's so-called modern history in 1916? Do we wish a nation weak, broken to pieces, irresolute, filled with conflicting and discordant voices, or do we wish a nation unified, strong, sympathetic, and ready to respond to the cause of a common purpose to serve all humanity, even though the rest of humanity be at war with itself?

The year 1916 is but one member of an infinite series. Countless eons have gone before it and countless eons will come after it. The physical forces of nature will go their way through indefinite time, performing their allotted functions, obeying their peculiar laws, and undergoing those manifold changes and transmutations which make up the heavens and the earth. Not so with the reputation and the influence of a nation. Opportunity will not knock forever at any door. It is knocking now at the door of the American people. If they are able to rise to an appreciation of their own part in the world, of their own controlling principles and policies; if they are able to put aside every self-seeking, every distracting, every brutal appeal, then no one can tell what light may illumine the page on which the history of our nation will yet be written.

It is nearly sixty years since Abraham Lincoln in his debates with Senator Douglas made much use of the Scriptural saying that "a house divided against itself cannot stand"; and he added, "I do not expect the house will fall, but I do expect the house will cease to be divided." So I say to-day to this influential company of Americans, we do expect, every one of us, that our house will cease to be divided. We do expect that our America will come to full consciousness of its purpose; that the serene courage of Washington, the constructive genius of Hamilton, the keen human insight and sympathy of Jefferson, the patient wisdom of Lincoln, will not have been in vain in teaching us what our country is and may become. Shall we catch sight of that something higher than selfishness, higher than material gain, higher than the triumph of brute force, which alone can lead a nation up to those high places that become sacred in history, and from which influence descends in a mighty torrent, to refresh, to vivify, and to inspire all mankind?

It is as true to-day as it was in ancient times that where there is no vision the people perish. We can make an America with a vision. We cannot make it without.

The nation must have a purpose. —

IX

NATIONALITY AND BEYOND

An Address delivered before the Commercial Club, San Francisco, Cal., August 8, 1916

NATIONALITY AND BEYOND

It is no small satisfaction to be able to stand for a few moments this afternoon in the presence of this great company of busy men, in order to discuss with them, however imperfectly, a matter which ought to be uppermost in the minds of every one of us.

Some weeks ago I was surprised and shocked to read in the public press the statement, attributed to a person of high importance, that with the causes and the outcome of the European War we Americans were not concerned. I am bound to assume that the words must have been used in some strange and unusual manner, for I find myself unable to believe that any intelligent American, in high station or in low, could hold the view which these words, interpreted literally, would appear to express. I should as soon expect one to say that we Americans were not interested in the revival of learning, or in the causes or outcome of the French Revolution, or in the invention of printing, or in the harnessing of science to industry, or in any one of the great, significant events in the history of free men. For unless I am wholly mistaken in the significance of these years through which we are passing, we are living in one of the great epoch-marking crises of the history of the world. We are standing at one of the watersheds from the heights of which streams of tendency and of influence will flow for generations, perhaps for centuries to come, now this way and now that.

What we are witnessing is not an ordinary international war. We are not spectators of a contest between Guatemala and Honduras over a boundary; we are standing before a struggle so stupendous, involving such incalculable sums of human treasure that all the great contests with which history is strewn fade into insignificance before it. This contest is not between savage and barbarous and untutored and backward peoples. It is not a strong barbarian who is emerging from the jungle to extend his reach over the less powerful. This war is a clash between ideals. It is a controversy over ideals and national purposes, and it takes rank with the most magnificent events in all history; and I use the word magnificent in its literal sense

of great-making, a great making-over of issues
and tendencies.

What we are witnessing is the end of the
old notions of Nationality. We are standing
at the bloody grave of an ideal that is a
thousand years old, one that has made the
history of Europe since the fall of the Roman
Empire. And we are witnessing the birth of
a new ideal, an ideal of Nationality with new
human significance, new human service, and
new human helpfulness—an ideal of Nationality higher than mere self-aggrandizement, or
economic wealth, or military power. This is
an ideal which calls to the heart and to the
mind of every American, and stirs his soul with
the hope and the desire that his nation may
participate in the upbuilding of a new conception of national purpose that shall call upon
us to see something in a nation that is beyond
population and wealth and trade and influence,
and that, whether the nation be great or
whether it be small, shall give it an honorable
place in the great structure which is civilization.

Just so long as every nation is regarded as
an end in itself, just so long will the world be

faced with the possibility of a recurrence of
this soul-stirring tragedy. Just so long will the
time come, at more or less frequent intervals,
when national ambition, national zeal, national
selfishness even, will find themselves struggling
for new and forceful expression, for new and
greater extension of influence, for new accomplishment and new grandeur.

I take it that the dream of one world-empire
has passed away forever. It was a dream that
came to the ancient Persians; it was a dream
that sent Alexander the Great with his troops
out over the deserts of Asia; it was a dream
that stirred the Roman conquerors; it was a
dream that gave Charlemagne his name; it was
a dream that showed us the magnificent spectacle of Napoleon trying to turn back the hands
of the clock of progress only a century ago.
That dream, I take it, has passed forever, and
we have now to deal not with the conception
of a world-empire, but with the conception of
clashing, conflicting, mutually antagonistic nationalities. International war at intervals is
the necessary accompaniment of that stage of
national politics. But magnificent as was the
diplomacy and the statecraft of those who

builded the present nations of Europe, that statecraft and the ideal of nationality which it pursued, have passed away forever. We are now coming to that state of international policy where, whether a nation be democratic or monarchical, informed public opinion matters mightily, and little by little is becoming the responsible controller of policy. An instructed and conscientious public opinion is reaching out to take the control of international policy out of the hands of monarchs and their irresponsible ministers, and to put that control in the hands of representative ministers of government who are responsible to their several peoples and who will no longer wage wars for personal, dynastic, or merely individual aims. As that democratizing of international relations, of foreign policy, takes place, the ground will be ploughed and harrowed and seeded and prepared for the crop of a new ideal. This is the ideal of a great community of nations each standing, as international law says it shall stand, as the equal of every other, whether great or small, powerful or weak, engaged in the common co-operative task of advancing the world's civilization, of extending its commerce and trade, of developing its science, its art, and its literature; all aiming to increase the standards of comfort, and to lift the whole great mass of mankind to new and higher planes of existence, of occupation, and of enjoyment. In that co-operative family of nations whose institutions are now in the making, there will be a place for every people, for every race, and for every language, and there will be a place for us. The compact of the Pilgrim Fathers on the *Mayflower*, the Declaration of Independence, the Constitution, the Gettysburg Address, and Lincoln's Second Inaugural are all one great series of steps in the development of our national purpose and of our international position and influence.

We are constantly reminded that George Washington counselled this nation to beware of entangling alliances that would carry us into the martial conflicts of Europe. We have wisely maintained that policy from his day to our own; but nothing was further from his thought than to counsel us against participation with every other nation in the solution of the great political problems common to all nations. We know, because their very names recall the knowledge to our minds, what the great nations of the ancient world and of modern times meant and still mean. We know what Italy means, what Germany means, what France means, what Holland means, what Great Britain means. We see with the eye of imagination their accomplishments, their service, and their great leaders of human influence and of action for centuries past. The question that now presses heavily upon our American people is, What shall we make America to be? Shall America come to be merely the symbol for a busy hive of industrious bees, or a symbol for a great hill of intelligent ants? Shall it mean only a nation absorbed in daily toil, in accumulation, in individual satisfaction, or shall it mean a nation so intelligent as to its purposes, so secure in its grasp upon its ideals and so devoted to them, that it will not rest until it has carried all round this world an American message that will raise and help and succor the stricken and conflicting family of peoples? Shall we keep to ourselves the great fundamental American accomplishments that have in them lessons for the whole world, or shall we use our influence to teach to others those accomplishments and to spread them abroad?

I mean, first, our literally stupendous achievement in federation. We have shown for the first time in history on a large scale that there may be flexibility in government combined with a single unit of ultimate control. We have shown how we can retain personal liberty and local self-government while building up a strong, powerful, united nation. Believe me, the world outside of the United States is waiting to profit by that experience. If there can be a common unity between Maine and California, Washington and Florida, uniting local self-government with membership in a great federated nation, why is not some part of that principle and why is not some part of that experience to be made ready for use and application by Great Britain, and Italy, and France, and Hungary, and Russia, and the rest?

Then, so many human conflicts arise out of differences of language, differences of religion, differences of institutional life, and so often the attempt has been made to suppress and to oppress the weak by the stronger. Men and women are told that they may not worship according to their faith; that their children may not be educated in schools where the vernacular is taught; and that there must be various differences between races and creeds and languages and types. Have we not proved to a watching world that the cure for that form of conflict is Liberty? Have we not shown that freedom of religion, freedom of education, equality of race and of language, letting all work out their several conflicts and controversies as they please subject only to the law, is the best policy? Have we not shown that out of these different elements, a strong, united nation can be built? And are we not ready and anxious to teach that to those who would still try to unify by suppression and by persecution?

Are we not ready as Americans first to set in order our own house, first to make sure that we ourselves are living at home in accordance with our ideals, with our best purposes, and are learning the lessons of our own experience? And then, shall we not be ready to say to Europe, to Asia, and to Africa, and to our sister republics to the South, that we feel our sense of international obligation? We have gained some information; we have proved some things. This information and this experience we offer them. We offer it in persuasiveness, in friendship, and in kindness. We offer this as our contribution to the great temple of civilization that we all would join to build.

What a day it will be, my fellow Americans, when we can take our Washington, our Jefferson, our Hamilton, our Marshall, our Webster, and our Lincoln out of the restricted class of merely American voices and American figures and American heroes, and give them to the world, to take their first place by the side of the great statesmen, the great artists, the great poets, the great seers of all time, as our contribution to a new civilization in which every nation shall find its place! Understanding this, let us press forward to a single goal for all men, the goal described and written in our own American Declaration of Independence.

That is the goal that lies beyond Nationality conceived as an end in itself.

X

THE PRESENT CRISIS

An Address delivered at a General Assembly of Columbia
University, February 6, 1917

THE PRESENT CRISIS

advancement for good ju[...]

There have been solemn and impressive moments in the life of this University, and there is a solemn and impressive moment now.

When the farmers at Concord Bridge fired "the shot heard round the world," the men of old King's College offered their services and their lives to the cause of national independence, and Hamilton, Jay, and Livingston went out of that little college to lay the foundations of a nation. In 1861, when Abraham Lincoln, patient, long-suffering, devoted to humanity, issued his call for 75,000 volunteers to repel the attack upon the integrity of the United States that was made in the firing on Sumter, the halls of Columbia College were almost vacant because of the company of students of that day who, with scores of the younger alumni, turned their faces toward the light. We are now facing a crisis in the history of our nation and in the history of mankind which will take its place by the side of the great crises that those who came before us met and faced, and

so gave this ancient college a reputation for
public service and for patriotic devotion that
justifies the splendid inscription on yonder
Library that it exists "for the advancement of
the public good."

The President of the United States, in formal
statement to the Congress, and through the
Congress to a listening world, has said that he
deemed it his duty to suspend diplomatic relations with the government of a great people to
whom we have long been bound by many and
close personal and intellectual relationships,
and to say that if there be an overt attack in
violation of public law upon an American right
he will have to ask the Congress for full authority to protect and to defend those rights by
whatever means may be found necessary. I
feel that I may with perfect confidence promise
to the President of the United States the unanimous support of Columbia University in that
great duty.

This is no light enterprise which we contemplate. Our people are sincerely devoted to
peace and would wish to walk in its happy and
fruitful paths with all their neighbors. But
there is something that they value more—and

that is liberty, justice, righteousness, and obe-
dience to public law. Upon those foundations
rest everything we are, everything we have
been, everything we hope to become, and every
service that we can render to mankind. Upon
those foundations rests the hope of the very
people who are now so madly warring against
them. In defending those great principles of
public order we are serving not the cause of
America alone, not alone the cause of those
who have so long and so valiantly carried on
the struggle on the battle-fields of this war, but
we are really serving the cause of those who,
for the moment, are blinded to the significance
of what they do.

Let no one say that if the President asks us
for service he is dragging us into a European
war and into conflicts as to national ambition
and national policy that are no concern of ours.
Nothing could be further from the fact. There
was no European war after the fateful hour
on the morning of August 4, 1914, when enemy
troops crossed the line of unoffending, innocent,
peace-loving Belgium. At that moment this
contest was lifted out of the area of a military struggle between dynasties and com-

mercial systems and ideas of government, and became a great epoch-marking world struggle as to whether public law and public right were or were not to be held superior to military necessity and to military ambition. That event made this war an American war, a South American war, a Chinese war, a Spanish war, an African war, a war on every man and every woman who hopes to live in freedom, in liberty, and in peaceful progress.

And now, after a patience so long continued and so unexampled that it has been doubtless misunderstood on both sides of the Atlantic, the President has summed up in clear phrase that can escape no intelligence just what is the situation on this fateful day. He will attack no one. He will voluntarily take no human life. He will voluntarily destroy no man's property. But if it comes to be a question as to the farther invasion of the people of the United States and their rights, then that people must act as one man in their defense· or cease to exist as other than a vassal state.

It may be—God grant it!—that this impending crisis may be avoided. But if it is not, the duty of every member of this University, man or woman, is perfectly plain. It is to say to the constituted authorities: "I am an American citizen; I am a son or daughter of Columbia; where can I be of use? What can I do? Where are my capacities, my strength, my training available? Can I use my skill on land, or on sea? Can I use it in civil administration, can I use it in supporting the needy, in relieving the suffering of those who are taken by military necessity from their occupations and their homes? Can I serve anywhere in the great army of peace-loving Americans who would only use force in order that right may speedily come to rule?"

Men and women of Columbia, let no one of you hesitate. Let no one of you draw back from this great obligation if it shall be laid upon you by our government. Remember that the stirring words of Mr. Lowell's verses upon "The Present Crisis," written before most of us were born, have direct and appealing application to you and to me to-day:

"Once to every man and nation comes the moment to decide,
In the strife of Truth with Falsehood, for the good or evil side;

Some great cause, God's new Messiah, offering each the
  bloom or blight,
Parts the goats upon the left hand, and the sheep upon
  the right,
And the choice goes by forever 'twixt that darkness and
  that light."

The opportunity to decide upon your patriotic duty will go as quickly as it may come.
Seize it for yourselves, seize it for your country, seize it for Columbia!

XI

IS AMERICA DRIFTING?

An Address delivered at the Annual Dinner of the
Chamber of Commerce, Pittsburgh, Pa.,
February 10, 1917

IS AMERICA DRIFTING?

He must be a poor and an unworthy American who is not stirred by the European War and its lessons to serious reflection upon problems affecting government and the future of civilization itself. This is no time to take things for granted. The great historic nations of the western world, those which have for two thousand years given shape and form and meaning to civilization and human progress, are shaken to their very depths. Experiences which might, under ordinary conditions, have extended over centuries, are being compressed into a few anxious and massively important years. No belligerent nation will emerge from this war on the same plane as that on which it was when the storm of war broke with such startling suddenness. Political institutions are being reshaped under the pressure of imperative national necessity with a speed and completeness that have no precedent in history. Economic and industrial relationships of long standing and great authority have already been overturned and revolutionized. New and grave seriousness of purpose, new and severe national self-examination, have taken possession of hundreds of millions of highly civilized people, who in the midsummer of 1914 were walking nonchalantly along the paths of history as unconcerned, as gay, and as self-centred as a maiden singing on a country road in summertime. The war has changed everything. Minor differences have fallen into insignificance. Even larger differences have been pressed into the background by the unifying force of stern national necessity and conscious national purpose. Despite their tremendous losses in men, in treasure, and in irreparable monuments, the chief belligerent nations will be found to have gained much from the terrible experiences of this devastating war. Their gain will be in the larger matters of national policy and in matters of the mind, of the spirit, of individual and national character. How is it with our neutral and aloof America?

When we turn our eyes from the battle-fields and council chambers of Europe to our own land, abounding in material prosperity and spared the terrible cost of military participation in the war, what do we find that in any way corresponds to the changes that have come over European opinion and European policy? Are we Americans learning the great lessons that the war has to teach, or are we so self-confident, so self-centred, and so self-opinionated that we think Europe has nothing to teach? Are we conscious of a distinct national purpose which commands our universal loyalty and devotion, or are we drifting on a sea of irresolution, divided counsels, and conflicting policies? It is worth while to examine this question from several different points of view.

Our representative men and our organs of opinion, both in high places and in low, are speaking and writing much of American participation in international affairs, of American guidance in shaping world policy, and of American aid in securing and in fixing the peace of the world. Are we prepared for these great undertakings? Are we so sure of our own ground, so firm and so clear in our opinions, and in our policies, so fortified in spirit and in material preparation, that we can confidently accept the challenge which the history of

Europe is making to our purpose and our competence as a nation?

It is a commonplace that democracies find it difficult to engage effectively in international intercourse. This is less true of a democracy like the French Republic, which has behind it a long national tradition, than of one like our own, which is even yet a newcomer in the family of nations that lead the world. Our form of government, with its division of power and responsibility between executive and legislature, between the nation and the constituent States, makes difficulties for the formulation and execution of a consistent international policy such as no other government in the world has to confront. Indeed, there are foreign nations that look upon the United States as in high degree irresponsible in international relations, so great are the obstacles which our temperament and our governmental forms put in our path as a nation. We do not generally recognize the fact that our form of government makes possible and our political habits make increasingly frequent the modification or repeal of explicit treaty provisions by a subsequent act of Congress, without any notice to the other high contracting power. We do not appear to take account of the fact that our form of government permits and our temperament encourages the denial by a State legislature or other local authority of rights secured to aliens by the solemn act of the treaty-making power. The government of the United States has bound itself by numerous treaties to give rights to aliens and to protect those rights. Despite this fact, the personal and property rights of aliens have been repeatedly violated in the United States, and our friendly relations with foreign countries have thereby often been put in jeopardy. The list of unfortunate happenings of this kind in recent years is a disagreeably long one. Within the memory of the generation now living, there have been outrageous attacks on aliens who were entitled by treaty to our protection, in Wyoming, in Washington, in Idaho, in Montana, in Oregon, in Alaska, in California, in Louisiana, in Texas, in Colorado, in Mississippi, and in Florida. It has been asserted that in the passage of the so-called La Follette Shipping Bill by the Congress at its last session, more than twenty treaties were rudely violated. So long as these conditions continue to prevail, we Americans live in far too much of a glass house to make it wise to throw stones at other nations who refer to a treaty as a scrap of paper. There are orderly and proper ways to modify or even to abrogate a treaty whose provisions are no longer sustained by American public opinion, and it is this orderly and proper way that should invariably be taken if we are to have and to exert permanent and beneficial influence in the council of the nations. A treaty is part of the supreme law of the land and must be respected and enforced as such.

If it be asked how are conditions to be bettered, the answer is, by a more intense, a more virile, and a more loyal nationalism. We must be Americans first, and citizens of a State or residents of a particular community afterward. We must give to the government of the United States, through the passage of legislation that has been recommended by Presidents Harrison, McKinley, Roosevelt, and Taft, the power which it does not at present possess, to protect the treaty rights of aliens through direct action in the federal courts. At the present time the federal officers and their courts have no power to intervene, either for the protection of a foreign citizen or for the punishment of those who commit an outrage against him. We must learn again for this generation and for the twentieth century the lessons of the Constitution and "The Federalist," the lessons of the Civil War and reconstruction. Americans must give up their increasing tendency to think in terms of classes, or groups, or sections, or States, and learn to think nationally in terms of the whole United States, its aims, its interests, and its honor. When America speaks or when America acts, the whole world should know that it speaks and acts as a nation and not as a series of conflicting and antagonistic groups or sections. When this comes to pass we shall have ceased to drift in our international policies and relationships.

If America is drifting in regard to matters of foreign policy, it is drifting, too, in regard to critically important matters of domestic concern. Our whole industrial system will be overturned with immense loss and damage to every interest unless we can agree upon a policy to reconstruct and remodel it on new and sounder lines. Our present habit is to let things drift until some acute crisis occurs, and then to meet it by surrender or by compromise, without any regard to the future, but with eyes fixed only on the immediate present. The greater part of the public seem to be utterly oblivious to the critical position in which the great railway systems of the United States have been put, not by constructive regulation or governmental supervision, but by policies of competing, conflicting, and unrelated persecution and pin-pricking. The great railways of the United States are national assets and they constitute the arterial system of our commercial and industrial life. They are asking and they should quickly receive, single, consistent, and well-ordered constructive oversight and regulation from the national government and from the national government alone. It was local interference with commerce that led directly to the formation of the Constitution of the United States. It is local interference with commerce that now constitutes perhaps our most difficult domestic problem.

Then, too, the time has come for us to acknowledge the primary obligation to the general public that rests upon every participant in any enterprise which is recognized as being invested with a public interest and which is to that extent under public supervision and control. If our national sovereignty is not to be surrendered to a group or an economic class, we must insist upon it that no public service shall be crippled or paralyzed by the concerted act of a group of individuals, taken without inquiry on the part of public officials into any alleged grievance, and carried on without regard to the overmastering public interests. In a peaceful and orderly economic state there are other modes of rebellion than insurrection in arms. It is for public opinion to recognize and to define these modes of rebellion against public authority and to find ways and means, just, kindly, and considerate, of dealing with them. When any individual citizen enters the service of the state, either directly or through some form of public service that the state regulates, he does so not through compulsion, but of his own accord, and he thereby assumes a kind and strength of obligation which does not necessarily rest upon his fellow, whose occupation lies outside of government or of government-regulated activity.

We should no longer hesitate to recognize

that every great industry and every great corporate undertaking is primarily something human, and not merely something mechanical, or material, or financial. It is not first of all an undertaking for gain, but it is first of all an undertaking in which human beings work together for purposes of joint and common interest. The traditional dogma of economists that the ultimate agents in production are land, labor, and capital, and the usual corollary that labor and capital have conflicting and mutually exclusive interests in the carrying on of an industry, have done an immense amount of practical harm. Leaving land aside, the essential elements in the production of wealth are all human beings and not dead abstractions to be spelled with a capital letter and treated as if they had neither flesh nor blood. It would be more accurate and more helpful if we were to classify the elements that enter into productive industry in threefold fashion: the man who works with his hands, the man who works with his head, and the man who works with his accumulations. Sometimes there is an overlapping of two of these classes, or in extreme cases even of all three of them, but, in general, each class represents a separate group in the industrial system. Each member of every such group should be made to have a common interest in their joint product.

It is sound economic and industrial policy so to organize industry that every co-operating element shall have a personal interest in its success and a personal share in its gains. There is, of course, a standard or prevailing rate of wage for the man who works with his hands, a standard or prevailing rate of salary for the man who works with his head, and a standard or prevailing rate of interest for the man who works with his accumulations. The man who works with his accumulations takes the greatest chance, because wages and salaries must of necessity be paid before his interest can be provided for. With a view to humanizing the great industries and to binding every worker more closely and more loyally to his undertaking, to giving him back some of that joy in the job that was characteristic of the hand-worker in the past, why should it not be agreed that, when the stockholders of a great corporation receive more than a fixed minimum of interest upon their investment, a similar distribution shall be made in terms of wages and of salaries to those who work with their hands and with their heads? Instead of an occasional bonus given as a favor at the end of a successful year, why should there not be a fixed percentage of salaries and of wages paid as a matter of right when the gains of an industry make it practicable? When there is an extra one per cent dividend to stockholders, might there not be an extra one per cent paid to those who receive wages and salaries? Under such a system every member of an industry, from the highest to the lowest, would feel a new pride in its increased productiveness, a new loyalty to it, a new interest in devices for saving time and eliminating waste, and a new satisfaction in increased profits. Why should we not leave off living on the edge of an economic and industrial volcano, waiting in fear and trembling until the next destructive and uncontrollable eruption shall occur, and settle down in relative peace and quiet, through the substitution of some such definite industrial aim as the one I suggest, conceived in human terms, for the policy of drifting which now governs so many of our economic and industrial relationships?

Such an aim would involve questions of housing, of health, of education, of recreation, of credit for long service, and those other attributes of decent living and good citizenship which are already so much on the mind of many great corporate organizations and their managers.

There is still another question that is dividing our people on which it would be easy to keep silent. It is, however, in my judgment, more honorable and more courageous for one who has convictions to speak them out. I refer to the question of preparation for national service under national control. No one can possibly hate the state of mind and the spirit that are militarism more than I do, and no one would resist more actively and emphatically any movement to change the peace-loving industrial spirit and temper of our people for any of the older forms of militarism that are now slowly going to their death, let us hope never to be resurrected, on the battle-fields of Europe. But there is a call to national service and a preparation for it which, so far from sharing the spirit of militarism, are only the voice of democracy conscious of its obligations and its duties, as well as of its rights and opportunities. We speak in general terms of the obligation which every citizen owes to his country, but what have we done to make that obligation precise and to fit each citizen to discharge it? What have we done to render more than lip-service to the democratic principle? Compulsion is not foreign to the spirit of democracy, although democracy uses it sparingly. Democracy lays its hands on the child, and for its own protection as well as for his good, says that he and his parents must discharge a certain obligation through attendance upon the elementary school. Social, economic, and political conditions are so varied throughout our land that the results of this policy are widely different and are in some ways far from satisfactory. This is not due to the fact that the policy itself is unsound, but because we have not yet learned how most wisely to administer it. Through compulsory attendance upon the elementary school the state endeavors to protect itself and each individual citizen from the dangers and limitations that attend illiteracy and the lack of all intellectual and moral discipline. In the light of our present experience, why should not the nation say to every youth approaching manhood: "We believe it to be in your interest and in ours that you should be required for a limited period in one year, or in each of two successive years, to subject yourself to definite, intensive, continuous training under national supervision and control, in order that you may first gain a new and vivid sense of the meaning and obligations of your citizenship, and in order that you may, in the second place, be physically and intellectually prepared to take part in your country's service, physical or military, should occasion for that use of your powers ever arise"? In our recent discussions we have been thinking too largely of national service and of preparation for such service in purely military terms. This is easy to understand, for the history of the past three years has forced it upon us as a people; but, if there were no war in Europe, and if there were no thought or need of preparation for war elsewhere, this need for the preparation of every male citizen for national service would be just as real and just as pressing as I believe it to be to-day. This question goes to the very roots of an effective and loyal and continuing democracy. It can be shirked if you will, it can be compromised if you will, it can be postponed if you will, but it can be neither shirked nor compromised nor postponed without damage to the life of the people of the United States. Why not leave off drifting and have a definite, conscious aim in our preparation for the full duties of citizenship?

We are drifting, too, in matters of public administration. Taking it all in all, our government is probably the most incompetent and most costly on earth. This is because it is so largely a government by those who talk, and that we have been so successful in excluding from it those who think and those who do. We pay enough in taxes, and far more than enough, to get thoroughly satisfactory administration of the public business; but we do not get this because competent administrators so rarely concern themselves with government or are chosen to responsible legislative or executive office. If the government of the United States were run in accordance with those principles which control the activity of any great non-governmental undertaking, from a steel corporation to a university, it would be the envy and the admiration of the world. I do not recall that any great administrator has ever been chosen to be President of the United States, and few governors or mayors seem to take any interest in the improvement of ordinary administration, such as every manager of an industrial or business undertaking concerns himself with every day and every hour. A man who had in his own person been successful and competent in the administration of a great business, whether it be a railroad, or a bank, or a manufacturing corporation, or a steamship company, or anything else, might, if elected to the presidency of the United States, accomplish a really wonderful service for our people. Four years, or even eight years, would be all too short to cleanse the Augean stables of waste and incompetence, duplication and inefficiency, which make Washington notorious, but eight years, or even four years, might be enough to make a beginning which would so appeal to the people of the United States that they would compel its continuance at the hands of any party which might happen to be successful in a subsequent election.

We are so concerned with our personal affairs, with our personal undertakings, and with our immediate interests that we are letting America drift. We give the feeblest possible support to the able and conscientious men who, here and there in the executive departments and in the national legislature, are doing their best to bear the heavy burden that has been put upon them. When such a man is sent to Washington, we leave him alone to fight our battles and his as best he can, and to face unaided the forces of stagnation, routine, and selfishness. Once every four years we arouse from our lethargy for a few weeks, and give more or less emotional expression to our aspirations and convictions; but when once the presidential election is over, we return to our several ploughs and America drifts again. What is everybody's business is nobody's business. Until every American feels his personal responsibility for the formulation of definite public policy at home and abroad, and for the businesslike administration of public affairs, America will continue to drift, and the rest of the world will continue to treat her as the spoiled child of the goddess of good fortune.

XII

LOOKING FORWARD

An Address delivered before the Commercial Club,
Cincinnati, Ohio, April 21, 1917

LOOKING FORWARD

This is a time when any one who rises to speak in public to his fellow Americans must do so with a feeling of heavy responsibility. There never was a time when there was so much that might be said; there perhaps never was a time when it was so difficult to say it freely, because the issue of the great struggle in which this world is engaged, despite all appearances, still trembles in the balance. An unfortunate or an unhappy sentiment publicly expressed even by a private citizen might be found to do great damage to the precious cause which every American and every citizen of the world has so closely at heart.

I remember the description which my father gave to me, such as your fathers must have given to many of you, of the state of feeling in this nation when Fort Sumter was fired on, and when the existence of this government, the integrity of the institutions that had been builded by the fathers, was suddenly put at stake. I confess to having had that kind of feeling when I read that enemy troops had invaded Belgium; and I confess to having had it in redoubled measure, and in a way that stirred every feeling and sentiment that I possess, when I read with you the awful news of the sinking of the *Lusitania*. There will not be years enough left in my life to dim the memory of the feelings which those events stirred in me, of the trains of thought which they opened, of the lines of policy which they suggested, of the great series of problems which from that day to this have been unrolled before the world. There is no use just now in looking back. The past has made its own record. It belongs to history. In the generations that are to come careful students of the documents will extract from the record, and put where all mankind may forever see, the precise story of the events that mark the cataclysm which began on August 1, 1914, and the end of which is not yet in sight.

That, I say, belongs to history; but we as Americans, as lovers of liberty, as citizens of the world, as lovers of our kind of every race and every speech, are concerned with what lies in front of us. We are concerned not alone with the national task but with the international happenings; and we are concerned not alone with the winning—the prompt, complete, and decisive winning—of this war; but we are concerned with the reconstruction of the political organization of the world that shall make place, ample place, for those people who are to-day our enemies, and at the same time prevent so far as human power and human foresight can prevent, the happening again of anything to be compared with this.

If we could imagine ourselves equipped with the modern press, the telegraph, the telephone, steam, and electricity, we might have been present at the fall of the Roman Empire and yet have witnessed nothing equal to this. We might under similar circumstances have been present over three hundred years at the Revival of Learning and yet have witnessed nothing comparable to this.

Every great struggle in this world is a struggle of ideas. Mere brute force is only the symbol of a wrong idea, or of a paucity of ideas. The struggle is in essence between ideas, and not always do those who are conducting it appreciate or realize that they are the bearers of the hopes or the hates of men. But when we look back to interpret the happenings of the past two thousand years, we see that in so far as the battle-fields of the world and the great military contests have not been purely dynastic, or personal, or predatory in character, they represented a conflict of ideas and of ideals.

Several times the history of this world has hung on the point of a spear. Each time the overruling Providence which guides and makes history has seen to it that the solution was toward the greater freedom, the greater progress, the greater liberty, the greater enfranchisement of man.

It was a very small group of men, comparatively, that landed from Persian ships on the immortal plains of Marathon; but if that little battle had gone differently the philosophy, the civilization, and the institutions of Asia would have made western Europe their own, and this continent would have been colonized fifteen hundred years afterward, if at all, by men who professed the philosophy, the politics, and the religion of those Asiatic peoples.

Time and time again, sometimes on a narrow field, sometimes in a mountain pass, sometimes at a Gettysburg, men have been thrown against each other in larger or in smaller mass, and the stake of victory was the world's policy or the life of a nation.

This controversy was apparently so simple in its origins—an ultimatum to Serbia, an answer, a declaration of war, a Russian mobilization, a German mobilization, a French mobilization, an invasion of Belgium, an English mobilization, and the world was in flames. Because that contest was apparently so simply begun, what was involved was hidden from the people of this nation. It has taken us two long years and a half to see that behind those struggling heroes that wear the uniform of France, and behind that great, silent, powerful British navy, were protected the Constitution and the laws of these United States. No war was being made on the Constitution and the laws of these United States; but war was being made on the ideas upon which that Constitution and those laws are based, and upon which alone they could be based and survive! This is therefore a war of high principle and in no sense a war of conquest. Let us never sing a hymn of hate to those who are for the moment worshipping a false god. A hymn of hate is just as unlovely when sung in English as in German. It is too solemn, it is too stupendous a controversy for hate; because if its issue be as we would have it, we shall lift another people to this high plane—a people at this moment in mighty arms against us.

Then we see what, at bottom? It is said that we see a conflict between autocracy and democracy, between despotism and liberty. We do; but we see something far more subtle than that. We see a conflict between two theories of politically organized man, one written in undying words in our own Declaration of Independence, that all governments derive "their just powers from the consent of the governed"; and the other based on the theory of a state all-powerful, unrestrained, superior to the limitations of law and morality, having a high end of its own which no power can restrain except by force, and which must sustain and extend itself by force. What is challenged in this contest is the Preamble to the Declaration of Independence of the United States.

That is why this has never been a European war. It began in Europe; but it never was a

European war. It might have been a European war if this country were a desert; but it could not be a European war so long as this country is concerned with ideas of government. The slow process of a glacier takes time; but you have seen in the heights of the Alps, or in our own northwestern mountains, its slow, creeping progress toward the overwhelming destruction of everything that stands in its way. This theory of an all-powerful, non-moral state, having its own rights self-given, not dependent on the just consent of the governed, armed with force and proceeding by might, would in time, unrestrained and unrestricted, like the glacier, have crept down the valleys of this western world and reduced them to sterile subjection to its might. I blame no individual human being for this war. I seek to bring no individuals to the bar of judgment, because I believe that ideas are so much more powerful than individuals that when they get those individuals in their grasp the latter are simply instruments of those stupendous forces struggling for the mastery of the mind and the conscience of man. It is that which we have been looking out upon. It is that which by

one happening and one act after another, here
a little, there a little, has brought this glacier
more and more close to the land on which we
stand, until finally the eyes of our people are
opened and they see that they are concerned,
deeply, nationally, and individually concerned
in this contest, because their ideals are at stake.

Why should we have taken so long? Why
should it have been hidden from us for two
years and a half, that this war was ours, was
all the world's; was a war on democracy and
liberalism in Japan; on the rising movement of
democracy and liberalism in Spain and the
South American republics, as well as on the
United States and every land where these ideals
are cherished; why should it have taken so
long? The answer hurts one to give. It took
so long because for a generation, with all our
changes and chances, we as a people have been
living in the lap of material luxury and gain,
and we had almost forgotten our soul. We
had almost forgotten the soul of this nation.

Turn back, when opportunity serves, to the
congressional and public debates and orations
of the first forty years of our nation's life.
There you will find the record of the spoken

words of men of every party, of every section, of all shades of opinion and belief; and through all their sentences and paragraphs there shines a soul. They knew that the body of this nation needed a soul to make it live. They had a clear conception of that soul, and they saw to it that this nation's body was given a soul.

We had almost forgotten our soul. We had apparently gotten to a point where we seemed to think that the world would go on no matter what we did; that somebody else would take care of liberty, somebody else would take care of justice, somebody else would take care of freedom, somebody else would take care of the open sea, somebody else would take care of the world's peace; and that we individually could go about our several businesses and let that "somebody" run the world! It cannot be done! No way has been found in a democracy of hiring Hessians to govern us; we must either govern ourselves, or drift on the tide of helpless serfdom to those peoples and those nations which are willing, as well as able, to govern.

Finally we have seen this vision; and now, thank God! the American people, conscious of

their soul, are hurrying to points of vantage
from which they can look forward. They are
sure of the past, and they are eagerly question-
ing the future, each according to his kind, as
to what it holds in store for men and for nations, and particularly for this dear nation of
ours.

I said a moment ago that even after these
two years and a half, and despite the happenings of recent weeks, the event still hangs in
the balance. It does. It hangs in the balance
for two reasons: first, no adequate means has
yet been found by any belligerent, or group of
belligerents, effectively to cope with the destruction of tonnage by the submarine. Sir
Edward Carson, the First Lord of the Admiralty, stated, speaking in the House of Com-
mons the other day, that in the time under
review forty combats with submarines had
taken place, and he left it to be inferred that
most or all of them had been successful; but
the fact of the matter is, as every man interested in the world's shipping knows, that with
the withdrawal of tonnage from commerce for
the customary purposes of war, with the lock-
ing up of tonnage owing to internment, high

rates of insurance, and danger from submarine
attack, and with the actual destruction of
tonnage which goes on week by week, it is not
yet certain that that particular mode of warfare will not prove even more powerful than
has been supposed. Let me give one illustration.

There has been comment and discussion as
to the relation of Italy to this war. Why has
not Italy, populous, well to do, with a large
and well-trained army, made more contribution to the allied cause through effective military operations? There are political explana-
tions into which I shall not enter; but I will
give you one economic explanation. Italy is
paralyzed from the mountains to the sea from
the lack of coal. Italy imports in normal times
ten million tons of coal a year. When the war
broke out the English government agreed to
furnish five million tons; and at once Italy had
to reduce by 50 per cent its coal consumption,
even at a time when an enormous increase was
demanded for the manufacture of munitions.
Now England has had to serve Italy notice
that no more coal can be delivered unless Italy
can provide the bottoms. That is a situation

which does not lie on the surface, but is one of the economic facts out of which the problems of this war have so largely arisen. I have cited that as one illustration, to which others might be added.

A second matter relates to Russia. If the provisional government of Russia is able to maintain itself, and if its army holds firm on the eastern front, there is every reason to believe that the war may be ended successfully within a reasonable time, say within the present calendar year. But if the morale of the Russian army is broken, or if by communistic outbreak such as took place in Paris in the winter and spring of 1871 following the German occupation, the hand of the provisional government should be paralyzed; if the Central Powers were to obtain possession of the agricultural and manufacturing resources of Russia, this war might go on for years.

To sit here in comfort and suppose that because these magnificent men of whose efforts we read with such anxious and joyous care every morning and every night, are doing such splendid things along the western front that there is nothing for us to do, that we can simply ride upon the field at the eleventh hour and share in the acclaim of the victors, is absolutely false. Nothing if persisted in could be more disastrous.

This one hundred millions of people has got to go to war. It will not do to saunter into war. It will not do simply to increase the income tax, to make a huge loan, and to read about war. War, with all its terrors, with all its horrors, with all its obligations, is on in this country, and our country's existence hangs in the balance. The American who cannot see that cannot read the plainest signs of the times; for even ideas, however powerful, however splendid, however noble, however uplifting— even ideas will not walk alone! Even ideas will not provide Italy with coal; even ideas will not cover the ocean with ships; even ideas will not grow a food supply adequate for this nation and for export; even ideas and speeches will not fulfil our obligations to those nations and those men who in darkness and in daylight have been fighting for your property and mine, for your government and mine, for your ideas and mine!

It is essential to the soul of the United States

that it should express itself in terms that history will not misunderstand. It is essential to the soul of the United States that we should make use, in the aid and interest of our fellows as well as of ourselves, of the great experience, the great opportunity, the great blessings, of the past century and a half.

We are trustees of a great and sacred trust. We have been given by Providence out of the womb of time this government with all its potentiality, with all its accomplishment, and with all its promise; and the question that comes home at this hour with burning force to every American is, how am I discharging my trusteeship? Not what is somebody else doing!—not what is somebody else doing! Not what is the President doing, not what is the Congress doing, not what is the French army doing, not what is the British navy doing— but what am I as trustee doing to preserve, to protect, and to perpetuate those ideals of government in which we not only believe as unassailable truths, but which we in our heart of hearts are convinced give the largest measure of promise to every people on this earth who will embrace them and make them their own.

We look, then, into the future clothed with a heavy and a solemn obligation; an obligation not simply to support the government—for that is conventional and banal—but with an obligation for personal service with head and heart and hand, in each and every one of those ways that shall contribute to the establishment of a just peace, durable because based on sound and lasting principles, a peace which will suppress and oppress no man and no nation, however it may be defeated in this war.

There are some things that follow from that argument as necessary corollaries. I should like to address myself for a moment or two to a contention frequently made in public that we have no concern with Europe, that we are isolated from its controversies and its contests, and that Washington himself, our most august American, specifically warned us against "entangling alliances." He did. But the most entangling alliance this nation could make would be an alliance with itself to cut itself off from the whole wide world! George Washington warned us against entangling alliances with individual nations against other nations—and he was right! We have never departed from

that counsel, and I see no reason in the history
of the intervening years, or in the outlook for
the future, to suppose that we should so depart.
But an alliance with one nation against another
nation is quite a different thing from standing
upright among our fellow men to bear our full
responsibility for the perpetuity of the world's
freedom and civilization. What sort of figure
should we cut in history if a thousand years
from now some far-off scholar looks back upon
us with his telescope and writes the history of
the twentieth century A. D., and finds a stupendous struggle for liberty, for the rights of
small nations, for the maintenance of public
law and treaty obligations, going on in Europe,
and a hundred millions of contented, self-sat-
isfied people sitting away across three thousand
miles of sea, and saying like the Pharisee of
old: "I am not as these men are, I am relieved
from any responsibility for what they may say
or do"? Our fathers came to this continent
to achieve something not for themselves alone.
Read every word they ever wrote. Read the
Declaration of Independence, read the Constitution, read those immortal words that can be
printed on the palm of the hand that were

spoken to you yonder at Gettysburg, and see whether that program of American policy is a selfish program, or whether it is a program of service to mankind?

No; steam, electricity, commerce, travel, finance, literature, science, the spread of ideas, the zeal for the very things that we believe in, have unified this round world into one family of nations, into one human society; and, as Mazzini said a generation ago: "Thank God, the philosophy of Cain has passed out of this world forever! We are our brothers' keepers." We are with them the keepers of an idea; and we can no more, in honor or in conscience or consistently with our history, shirk this responsibility than we can give the lie to our spoken word or written bond; far less so, for that would be a personal failing and a personal crime or sin, while this would be a great public crime committed in the forum of human history and in the full sight of every immortal soul that has gone before, and would continue to be so regarded by every human being that remains to be born upon this earth. We dare not, gentlemen, we dare not!

We have ourselves in our earlier public policy

done nobler things than that. Our fathers, and our fathers' fathers, were in the closest relation with the political and international happenings of Europe. What about the influence of Benjamin Franklin, of Thomas Jefferson, of John Quincy Adams, of Chancellor Livingston, of Henry Clay, and of the whole series of great men who laid the foundations on which we are building bit by bit the superstructure?

Do not forget that the name that has most enchained the hearts of the people of the United States next only to Washington and Lincoln themselves, is the name of La Fayette. When he came back, an aging man, to visit the country that he had helped to save and to make, his was a triumphal progress from capital to capital and from city to city. I venture to say that at this moment there are probably more counties, towns, and villages in the United States that bear the name of La Fayette than bear the name of any other human being. That testifies to the relationship a century ago. When Kossuth, the Hungarian liberal and revolutionist, came to this country, everything was done to welcome him to the United States because he was rebelling against a tyrannical government at home. Those fathers felt the electric spark of sympathy with an idea; and they did not hesitate to give it expression in the written and the spoken word.

No, gentlemen, what cut us off from our just relations to the civilized world was our own unhappy division over slavery, and the resulting war between the States. That was the knife which severed the bond that had from the very beginning united us in sympathy and in understanding to the older civilization. What we are doing now is not for an instant anything new, not for an instant anything revolutionary. We are repairing the damage wrought by that great civil dissension; we are going back to our just place as lovers and recognizers of liberty, and showing ourselves ready and willing to stretch a hand across any sea to those who battle for our ideas, and therefore for us! That is traditional American policy.

Let no man who has only read fifty years of American history, who has only seen the curtain that we let fall between the two acts, attempt to introduce us to the subject-matter of the drama. The drama, the great world drama, goes on everlastingly. Our relation to it is a matter for our intelligence and our conscience and our sense of high principle. Do you realize that the world owes to us—looking now to the credit side of the account for a moment—do you realize that the world owes to us very much of the progress which had already been made toward international organization when this war broke out? The great importance in history, in American history, of the two Hague Conferences of 1899 and 1907 does not seem to be generally recognized. The Conference of 1899 was called by the Tsar of Russia to discuss disarmament. The United States was represented by a distinguished delegation. When the nations assembled at The Hague they soon discovered through interchange of views on the part of their representatives that disarmament was impossible and impracticable. They discovered what any man, I think, who examines that question candidly will discover, that armaments, while the instruments of war, are not the causes of war, and that to take away the instruments and leave the causes would mean to expose this world to still more dreadful, still more costly, still more inhuman wars. Therefore, they said: "We cannot dis-

arm; let us adjourn." The American delegation said: "No; do not adjourn. Cannot we
do something, make some slight progress toward
the prevention of war? Cannot we take some
step that will make these tremendous outbursts
less likely?" And the project was brought forward for a Court of Arbitration. It was dis-
cussed for some time; it was accepted by France
and by Great Britain, and by other nations;
it was strongly opposed by the representatives
of the German Empire. Then happened this:
Doctor Andrew D. White, *clarum et venerabile
nomen*, the senior member of the American
delegation, formerly Minister at the Court of
Berlin, wrote a personal letter to the German
Emperor and pleaded with him for the sake of
the future to instruct the German delegates to
alter their attitude. That letter was intrusted
to the secretary of the American delegation,
the late Frederick W. Holls, unfortunately gone
from earth all too soon to render the splendid
services to the better organization of the world
of which he was capable. In a two days' interview with the German Emperor and Prince von
Buelow, Count von Buelow as he was then,
that letter of Doctor White's, aided by the

personal influence of Mr. Holls, brought about instructions from the German Emperor to the German delegation at The Hague to change their attitude. They did change it; and the first Court of Arbitral Justice was established. The United States made that contribution toward the better organization of the world. Some day that letter of Doctor White's will be seen to have been an epoch-making one in the history of American diplomacy and in the history of international organization. Then the Conference adjourned. There were those who said in America and in Europe: "The Conference has been a failure. Why try to put life into this chimerical idea?" But the President of the United States, Mr. Roosevelt, hurried before that court the Pious Fund case between the United States and Mexico, and gave an impressive lesson to the world of two sovereign nations submitting a claim involving their sovereign rights to the decision of five private gentlemen in black coats at the Dutch capital. Again the United States had made a powerful contribution to the organization of the world.

A few years ago it was my privilege to sit for a time in the Court at The Hague, and I saw what I shall always remember as one of the most impressive sights of my life. Five gentlemen entered at ten o'clock, as they might in any American appellate court, took their places upon the bench, and without any more ado counsel rose in his place and commenced his argument. The counsel was Elihu Root, Senator from the State of New York, presenting the case of the United States of North America against Great Britain in regard to the Newfoundland fisheries; a case which had brought the two countries involved to the verge of war a dozen times in the century. He presented it as quietly, in as lawyer-like fashion, as if he were arguing in the Circuit Court of Appeals or before the Supreme Court of the United States. He was followed after a time by opposing counsel, the Attorney-General of England, who rose in his place to present the opposing argument. Days, weeks, went by; the exhibits and the testimony were submitted, argument was heard, the court rendered its decision, and the Newfoundland Fisheries case between Great Britain and the United States disappeared from the history of trouble-making diplomacy, after having occupied a prominent place in it for a century. Again the United States had made a powerful contribution to the better organization of the world.

And then it was urged that The Hague Conference should be convened again. The Reactionary party in Russia were in power; they kept the Tsar from calling it. The President of the United States, at that time Mr. Roosevelt, gave notice that if the Tsar did not call it, he would. The Tsar called it! The Second Hague Conference assembled in 1907; and there this Court of Arbitration, which was really not a court in the strict sense of the word, but a body of diplomatic negotiators not bound by law, but trying to arrive at an agreement by mutual consent, concession, and yielding, gave way to the idea of a real court, an International Court of Justice. This project was presented on the instructions of the Secretary of State of the United States, Mr. Root, through the American delegation headed by Mr. Choate. When Mr. Choate rose to present that argument before The Hague Conference, he opened by saying: "We have now spent weeks in regulating the laws of war; can we not spend a few hours in trying to prevent war?" And he brought forward the plan which after weeks of discussion was agreed to as a satisfactory plan. The Hague Conference then adjourned without a constituted court only because the small nations and the great could not agree as to how the judges should be appointed in the first instance. That was the condition when the present war broke out.

Remember that this proposal for a genuine International Court has been assented to by Great Britain, by Germany, by France, by Austria, by Italy, by Russia, by Japan, and by the United States; and there it stands. And when this war is over, that is the point at which we should begin; we should resume our constructive work at the point at which this war broke it off. We can say, as no other people in the world can say: "We can give you out of the whole of our experience with the one hundred and twenty-odd years of the Supreme Court of the United States, an example of just how this institution will work, just what problems will arise, just how it has been found satisfactory to settle them between the first thirteen and now forty-eight sovereign States of the American Union."

I will not go into detail. The international organization of the world is a most fascinating subject. Few of us know how far it has proceeded. When this war broke out there were about two hundred and fifty international organizations that had their seat of business at Brussels, dealing with every sort and kind of activity, commercial, industrial, scientific, literary, governmental, and behind them all lay this great conception of an international judicial process.

Now what is required for the carrying out in the future of that great American policy? Two things are required: first, the supremacy in the world of the rule of law, and the suppression forever, if possible, of the rule of might. There is needed that good-will among men which is the only final sanction of public action. Forms of organization will help, but they alone will not suffice. Legislation may help, but it will not accomplish. The real problem before America and the world, the problem that stares us in the face as we look forward is, how to secure for ourselves, how to spread abroad among others, that belief in law and order, and that good-will which will

put blood and nerves and life, body and brain,
into a great legal organization that the nations
may agree to work under.

That is your problem and mine; that is the
problem of the Frenchman, of the Briton, of
the Italian, of the German, of the Russian, of
the Bulgarian, of the Japanese, and the rest.
Order, peace, prosperity, cannot be imposed on
this world by might. A temporary victory of
that kind would mean a new outbreak of the
irrepressible spirit of liberty as soon as it could
catch its breath after its defeat. The temporary triumph of might would mean indefinite
wars on this earth: for the men upon it are facing the front; they are looking for the light;
and they are not going because of the fine
phrases of a false philosophy to put upon their
minds and upon their bodies the shackles that
it has taken hundreds of years to strike from
the limbs of their ancestors.

So, gentlemen, many as are the outlooks upon
the future, that is the one which looms largest
to me, that is the one which it seems to me
has the most significance for each one of us.
There are others vitally important. You must
have observed with what speed the necessities

of war have caused the complete social, industrial, and financial reconstruction of great nations. The Great Britain of 1914 does not exist; there is a new Great Britain of 1917. The France of 1914 does not exist; there is a new France of 1917; and the United States of 1914 does not exist, and never will exist again! There is a new United States beginning to be born. A whole series of economic problems that have been intrusted by us to individual initiative and competition are in these European countries already, and in our own country to-morrow, to be cast in a new form where they are to be approached by men in association with each other and with government.

That change has in it an element of strength and an element of danger; but whatever elements it has, here it is. If this reorganization in Great Britain, in France, and in America, proves effective, as it bids fair to, in ending this war successfully, the populations of these countries will never wholly desert it even in times of peace. Therefore, we must be prepared for a new outlook upon our industrial and commercial life. We must expect to find that we are called on for a far larger measure of co-operation and subjection to control than ever before. If that can be accomplished without destruction of individual initiative, without depriving the individual of the just rewards of his endeavor, without reducing all men to the common level of mediocrity, it will have in it elements of progress, of success, and of happiness. If, on the other hand, it proves simply to be a new chain under the guise of an invitation to liberty, we shall find ways and means of loosening it; because, gentlemen, the one thing that will not be kept down, the one thing that no power can forever control, is the desire of the human heart to be free; free to think, free to express itself under ordinary and just limitations that fix the equal rights of others; free to labor; free to maintain itself in possession of its just gains. Because we know that if we surrender that, we again exalt an all-powerful state above the individual, and then it is not long before we shall pay tribute to it as possessing those mysterious powers which are but the symbol of might and tyranny.

There are dangers in success; there are dangers in the very solutions that are proposed of the problems that will lead to success; but if we look all these problems in the face, if we understand them, if we keep our heads clear, our tempers in control, we may be able to surrender what is needed, to do our just part, without impairing those fundamental things in which we all so profoundly believe and which are at stake in this war.

There could be no more cynical conclusion of this war than for those of us who are allies to defeat the German army on the field of battle, to surrender in the process to the ideas that have taken the Germans captive and sent them into this contest. It is as necessary for us to defeat the spirit of might and militarism in our own hearts and in our own land, in our own economic and industrial organization, as it is to prevent it from conquering on the field of battle. That is the dilemma, that is the difficulty, which confronts us.

So here we stand, looking out across this troubled and dangerous sea to those who are for the moment protecting us; making ready, let us hope as speedily as may be, and in all possible ways, to give them support, and to join them as we should with our flag, our ships, and our men.

We are looking across the sea, facing not only war but problems of life, problems of conduct, problems of political and economic organization. It will be a supreme test of the capacity of the American people to rule, not others but themselves, and to control, not dependents, but their own interests; to keep their place without losing it, and to take their just place without pushing aside any other human being who is entitled to the same rights that we claim for ourselves.

XIII

THE RUSSIAN REVOLUTION

An Address delivered at a Meeting of the National
Institute of Arts and Letters at the Hudson
Theatre, New York, April 23, 1917

THE RUSSIAN REVOLUTION

I could wish that this honorable and difficult task had fallen into other hands than mine. The story which Mr. Kennan has just recited out of the wealth of his experience, his observation, and his participation is but one chapter in the long record of political and civil crime that so stirs one's blood and so causes one's gorge to rise that it is difficult to speak in this public presence, as one should speak, with restraint and yet with appropriate feeling and appreciation. For myself, the events of these last months and years are so much the most important happenings in two thousand years of history that I find it difficult not only to speak of them, but to think of them, without constant use of superlatives, without those comparisons and that emphasis which often destroy by their very strength. And of all these events, of all these happenings, what more stupendous than the spectacle of a great national giant, that stretches its huge limbs over a seventh of the earth's surface and includes in its population nearly two hundred millions of human beings, rising to the full stature of a free nation in the midst of a world at war, with every danger internal and external threatening, and yet with the sacrifice of fewer lives than Mr. Kennan's censor would have sent to the gallows or to prison in a single month? This is the triumph of an idea! The men of letters and the artists gathered here, who are devoted to the expression in their several media of an idea and an ideal, are the first and the quickest to recognize the significance of what has happened.

What has happened is not the framing of a constitution; none has yet been drawn. What has happened is not the success of an armed revolution; there has been none. What has happened is not what happened at Whitehall in January, 1649, or what happened in the Place de la Concorde in January, 1793; for that has not happened. What has happened is that an idea, slowly germinating in the mind of a great people who have been set off by language, by religion, by custom, by barriers of geography from a great portion of the western world, has given birth to a new political era for that people and has moved the boundary between East and West from the Vistula nearly to the Yellow Sea.

The great Slavic nation has thrown in its lot with the West. It has given expression to the idea which makes the West, the idea which one day will make the newest West out of the whole of the immemorial East. That idea is the product of philosophy and of letters. That idea has called into being the great master-pieces of the poet, of the writer of imaginative prose, of the historian, of the seer, of him who works in plastic materials, bending them to spiritual and intellectual forms. That idea is the idea of human liberty. There have been attempts—how numerous it would be common-place to mention—to hold it in check, to keep it back; but like a great, all-powerful, slow-moving, fateful glacier it has come down from its fastnesses in the human heart and the human soul, watered by the perpetual snows of human aspiration, until it is conquering, not for destruction but for fruitfulness, all the green valleys which lay spread out before its path.

Perhaps the most potent force in this world to-day is the force of a man of letters who has been dead for one hundred and forty years, a man whose philosophy was absurd, whose knowledge of history was negligible, whose character was grotesque, whose contradictions were almost as numerous as his utterances. But the reason why Jean Jacques Rousseau put force and life into the American, the French, and the Russian revolutions was that with all his limitations, with all his oddities, he preached the gospel of human liberty in ways that ordinary men and women could read and understand. If we look back across the troubled generations that lie between him and us, we must forgive him for his faults, for his absurdities, for his crudities, and take note only of the fact that the idea which he was moved to put into so many different literary forms had about it such power, such charm, such immortality, that it is carrying his name at this moment around the earth as one of the effective makers and shapers of this spiritual rebirth of the Slavic people. Rousseau was a man of letters; and we celebrate this far-off genius in this last act, this latest expression, of the current of thought which he did so much to direct. For he had not originality enough to invent or to discover it; he had simply the power to make it take hold of men and women of different speech, of different lands, of different race, of different traditions.

The centre of gravity of the world's interest has shifted, and we now see as we could not see a year ago the real meaning of the great military struggle that is engaging the manhood and the wealth of the world. As a struggle between autocracy and liberty it was anomalous so long as the Tsar and Autocrat of all the Russias was found in the ranks of liberty; but now that his people have thrown off the domino which they have worn for three hundred years, they stand out in their true uniform as another struggling democratic people, marching upward toward the light.

Those of us who remember our history must be careful not to let our enthusiasm outrun our judgment. A great thing is happening; but it has only just begun to happen and there are many obstacles, many difficulties, many possibilities of error and delay in the path. See how long it has taken the English-speaking peoples to build their institutions, and how anxious they still are to improve them. See how long it took France, even after her revolution had begun, to establish on firm foundation and with common consent a Third Republic that was safe from internal corruption and damage. We must not expect Russia to do at once what it has taken England, America, and France generations and even centuries to accomplish. The very autocracy under which Russians have lived has deprived them of much of the stimulus and the material for swift institution-building. Yet they have come late, and they so have the advantage of the experience, of the errors as well as of the successes, of those of us who have gone before.

One lesson the Russians will learn if they look us straight in the face, if they look England, and France, and America straight in the face; and that is that liberty does not mean license, but discipline. Liberty means self-discipline; it means reaching out with the hand of history and the hand of philosophy and the hand of observation and taking into oneself and making one's own those principles of conduct, personal and political, those forms of organization, civic and social, which history justifies and which the conscience of mankind approves. That is self-discipline, the self-discipline of an individual and the self-discipline of a nation. No nation, old or young, Latin or Slav, Anglo-Saxon or Teuton, will ever be free until it disciplines itself. To insist upon that fact, is perhaps the greatest service we can render our newly emancipated friends across the sea and across the warring lands that lie between. When we welcome them to the sisterhood of free self-governing nations, let us not welcome them without some fair warning as to our difficulties and problems, without some suggestion as to the obstacles that lie in their path, that they may not make the mistake that some have made who have gone before in thinking that a revolution is effected by a single turn of the human wheel. The mere abdication of a Tsar does not constitute a democracy.

When the present revolutionary movement took its rise with the general strike and the massacres of twelve or thirteen years ago, an American observer journeyed to Russia to take note of the happenings. In a conversation with Tolstoy he said that he had come to remain a year or two to study the Russian revolution.

Tolstoy said: "Come prepared to stay for fifty years." Tolstoy was right. We are only at the beginning of a great public movement which follows upon a hundred years or more of a preparation which we in the western world have not fully understood. The village community life of the Russian people has long given training, excellent, admirable training, in the affairs of government and domestic economy to thousands and tens of thousands of peasants with whom reading and writing are arts yet to be acquired. The Zemstvos, called into existence fifty years ago, have grown in experience and authority until as provincial assemblies they have taken on some of the attributes of an American State legislature. During the past two and a half years they have been the most effective single instrument in equipping the Russian people to carry on the war, not only in a military but in an economic sense. There again, thousands and tens of thousands of peasants have been trained in habits of cooperation, in methods of government, in methods of accomplishing public ends through public acts, all of which are strangely different from passing resolutions and issuing manifestoes. And so when the time came and the domino could be thrown aside, it was not to a wholly untrained and unfamiliar people that this opportunity for self-government came. It was rather to a people already partially tutored in government and to one whose members had long, long been thinking hard about government. If that under which they lived was government, what could governments be for? Can you wholly fail to understand the men who could only answer Mr. Kennan's category of crime by violence? Among one hundred and seventy millions of people is it strange that there were some who could not wait? Is it strange that there were some who could not control their passions and who, stirred to the deepest resentment by what they saw and felt and suffered, gave way, human-like, to those passions which could only aggravate although intended to cure? It is not strange. There is a point beyond which human nature cannot resist temptation, and that point was reached, long ago reached, under the autocracy of Russia.

Now, I repeat, the centre of gravity of the world's interest has changed. We follow with the greatest anxiety the daily, almost the hourly, movement of those magnificent armies that are standing between the American people and their foes on the western front in Europe. But the future of the new Europe, perhaps the future of humanity, is being worked out to-day while we sit here, on the unfamiliar banks of the Neva, the Volga, and the Vistula. If Russia holds firm, if her new-found political consciousness and her new-found political power stand the storms from within and without to which they certainly are exposed, the successful end of this war for liberty is in measurable sight. But if Russia gives way and if the whole of the eastern continent is open to those who hold other views and have other aims than ours, this war may last till every head in this hall is gray. On Russia, on free Russia, on democratic Russia, now depends the early and the successful issue of the war.

Must we not then, men of letters, artists, citizens, hasten to the highest mountain-top and call out our greeting across land and sea to those who would stand with us for this common cause? Should we not hasten to call out to them a word of encouragement and help and warning, and to say: "We understand what you have gone through; we know what the past has been. Stand firm, and help us to make a new future that will be a new future for the United States as well as a new future for Russia"?

Years ago, in a striking statement, Count Muravieff said Russia was coming to bear upon her shoulders the new age. "We are coming," this is his phrase, "to relieve the tired men." The Latins have had their great era; the Anglo-Saxons have had their great era; the Teutons have had their great era; and now the Slav emerges into the full view of modern history and into participation with it to relieve the tired men. The Slav is going to come with all his unknown potentiality, with all his amazing differences from what have hitherto been the western peoples. The Slav is going to come, bound to the west by this new social and political ideal and by this possession of new social and political power.

Long ago, three quarters of a century ago, Gogol looking out on his land cried: "Whither art thou speeding, my Russia?" Now we think we have an answer to the question.

Whither art thou speeding, Russia? Speeding toward the high places that are in possession of those human spirits who love liberty, who love justice, who preach and who practise righteousness, and who, with all their faults and stumblings and imperfections, will labor for the coming of that happy day when this earth shall be a better place to live in because men are all free and just together. That is where we must hope that Gogol's Russia is speeding.

XIV

THE CALL TO SERVICE

An Address delivered at the Service of Farewell to
Columbia Students Leaving for the War,
St. Paul's Chapel, Columbia Uni-
versity, May, 6, 1917

THE CALL TO SERVICE

In all the long and honorable history of our University, there has been no hour just like this. The world is at war, and this University, in common with the nation that it loves and serves, is about to send of its bravest and its best to take a share in a struggle on whose result the history of mankind for centuries will hang.

On the eve of that going out, we gather to participate in this stately and solemn service to Almighty God, in Whose name this University was founded and in Whose name it has labored from generation to generation.

This hour, these happenings, this service, bring us face to face with the everlasting values of life, and with a contemplation of those standards by which men measure conduct and civilization and by which history awards them praise or blame. While we are here in quiet contemplation and prayer, on the other side of the Atlantic, at this very moment, more than twenty million men in arms are struggling to determine whether our nation and our University shall live.

On the northern and eastern slopes of Vimy ridge, on the uplands of Craonne looking upon the historic fortress of Laon over territory which has been the scene of historic contest since the days of Julius Cæsar, your fate and mine is being determined by men whom we have never seen and whose very names we do not know. And then, away over yonder beyond the Vistula and the Masurian Lakes, on down across the Balkan peninsula to the very gates of the garden of Eden itself, participants in this struggle are face to face in arms.

The call for liberty, for righteousness, for justice between men and nations, has filled the ears and stirred the hearts of our nation, and this University has responded in the only way that a university of its traditions and ruling principles could respond. Without boastfulness, without vaunting, but with quiet and serene courage and determination, our every member will take his place as soldier or civilian in that great army of the people which is enlisted to bring this war to a speedy and final conclusion on such a basis that just peace may reign in this world, and, in the fine phrase of the President, "the world may be made safe for democracy."

Columbia gives all it has, and it is with infinite pride and brotherly satisfaction that we look into the faces of this youth which has elected to enroll in the military service of the United States and to place its intelligence, its character, its training, at the service, not alone of its country, but of the great fundamental principles on which civilization rests.

One of the oldest and subtlest philosophies in the world teaches that the whole of history consists in the struggle between the principle of good and the principle of evil. It teaches that now one, now the other, is uppermost, but that as the good principle overcomes the evil, or as the evil principle overcomes the good, so mankind marches forward to freedom or so it falls back into serfdom and slavery.

This great struggle between the good and the evil principle has taken, in this twentieth century, the form of a contest between two political and social principles which cannot live together in this world. And that is why this contest must be settled by force of arms.

If those two principles had anything in common, an adjustment between them might possibly be reached; but each principle absolutely excludes the other. As Abraham Lincoln said a generation ago, "This nation cannot exist half slave and half free," so it may be said to-day, "This world cannot exist half despotism and half democracy."

Democracy must in its way dispose of despotism or despotism will in its way overcome democracy. Therefore, it is to no ordinary contest that this nation goes forward. It is to no struggle as to which one may be for a moment indifferent. It is to the deepest and most tremendous conflict that all history records, and Columbia answers, *Adsum!* Columbia stretches forth her hand in preparation to aid those of her sons who are rushing forward to posts of honor and service and danger, and then extends her hand in blessing and benediction upon them and their ideals and their efforts.

Wherever the cause of liberty is in danger, there Columbia's hand will be found to help avert it. Wherever the rule of despotism is extending, there Columbia's hand will be found to remove it. Wherever there is need of scientific skill and genius to serve, to cure, to invent, to construct, there a Columbia hand will be found ready to do its duty for the advancement of the public good and for the glory of Almighty God.

XV

THE ENVOYS AT THE UNIVERSITY

An Address delivered at a Special Convocation of
Columbia University, May 10, 1917

THE ENVOYS AT THE UNIVERSITY

Since in 1861 Columbia University gave its highest honors to Abraham Lincoln, it has known no such day as this. In the modern democracies, the university—and the university almost alone—is able to rise above strife of party or of faction, above difference of religious creed, above official forms and material standards, to speak for the spirit and the mind of the whole people. This University is especially competent so to speak because of its long and noble tradition, because of its unbroken record of distinguished public service, and because of the great army of men who from decade to decade, and now even from century to century, have gone out through its gates to serve the State and to play a man's part in the world. To-day this University speaks with no uncertain voice to offer a welcome, finely symbolized by the outstretched arms of Alma Mater, to those great men who, as captains of the public policies of democratic peoples, as captains of armies and of navies, and as cap-

tains of commerce and of finance, have represented with consummate skill and supreme
devotion the aspirations and the purposes of
the French Republic and of the British Empire. It is in but a superficial sense that
France, Great Britain, and the United States
are allies in the conduct of war; in a far deeper
sense they are companions in the great enterprise of democracy, in the spreading of higher
hope and broader opportunity among men, and
in the upbuilding of a yet finer and fairer and
more secure structure of civil and political liberty upon the foundations that the fathers have
laid.   The intellect and the conscience of America, speaking so far as they may by this University—the University of Alexander Hamilton, friend and companion-in-arms of La Fayette—cry Hail to these representatives of our
brothers, and bid them know how complete and
how whole-hearted are our country's understanding of their aims and our country's appreciation of their accomplishments and their
sacrifices.   Behind the powerful defense of
their armies and their navies we have for two
and a half years rested secure and undisturbed.
The time has fortunately come when the Ameri-

can people have declared their purpose to add might to their sympathy and to put determination behind their good will. To this epochal fact full testimony is borne by the city of New York, the great power-house of the nation's energies, in which is centred so much of American activity and from which radiate so many of the directing forces in American life.

There can be but one certain end to this war, and there can be but one road to durable peace. Were it possible to contemplate the present victory of those forces that would halt and imperil democracy, there would lie before us, before our children, and before our children's children, an unbroken series of wars, until those who come after us had gained what we in our day had failed to accomplish. The upward progress of mankind may be delayed or checked, but it cannot forever be prevented. In the whole course of history, no great crisis which involved the forward march of man has been resolved to his disadvantage. Democracy will win this war because the works of men will not fall below the full measure of their faith.

To you, M. Viviani, representative of the government and the mind of France; to you,

Marshal Joffre, whose name and fame already belong to the ages; to you, Lord Cunliffe, as a tower of national strength; and to you, Mr. Consul-General, representing the Right Honorable Arthur James Balfour, consummate flower of British cultivation and British statesmanship—I bid sincere and affectionate welcome to this University, which, as yonder legend reads, was "founded in the Province of New York by Royal Charter in the Reign of George II, perpetuated as Columbia College by the people of the State of New York when they became free and independent, maintained and cherished from generation to generation for the advancement of the public good and the glory of Almighty God."

XVI

THE INTERNATIONAL MIND: HOW TO
DEVELOP IT

Introductory Address delivered at the National Conference on Foreign Relations of the United States, held under the auspices of the Academy of Political Science, Long Beach, New York, May 28, 1917

THE INTERNATIONAL MIND: HOW TO DEVELOP IT

For two generations it has been a common complaint that the people of the United States took no adequate interest in foreign policy, and were without any but cursory knowledge of international politics. This judgment has been expressed, often publicly, by successive secretaries of state, by those who have held important diplomatic posts, and by those who, in the Senate of the United States, have seen long service upon the Committee on Foreign Relations. A sort of national self-centredness together with a feeling of geographic and political isolation have combined to bring about this unfortunate state of affairs. It has been unfortunate for two reasons: first, because it marked a serious break with our earlier national tradition; and second, because it has held back the people and the government of the United States from making the full measure of contribution of which they were capable, to the better and closer international organization of the world.

One need have but slight acquaintance with
the writings and speeches of the fathers and
with the records of the early Congresses to
know that, when the government of the United
States was young, it was the eager ambition of
those who most fully represented it to play a
large part in the international life of the world,
primarily with the view of advancing those
ideas and those principles in which the people
of the new American republic believed and to
which they were committed.   Benjamin Franklin was our first great internationalist.   Alexander Hamilton, of whom Talleyrand said that
he had divined Europe; Thomas Jefferson,
whose public service in Europe was quite ex-
ceptional; as well as Chancellor Livingston,
John Jay, Charles Cotesworth Pinckney, John
Quincy Adams, and Henry Clay not only knew
western Europe, but were known by it.   In
making endeavor, therefore, to increase the
interest of the American people in foreign relationships and in international policy we are
but asking them to return to one of the finest
and soundest of national traditions.

Our national self-absorption has held us
back, too, from playing an adequate part in

the development of that international organization which has long been under way and
which the results of the present war will hasten
and greatly advance. Despite these facts, and
chiefly because of the high character and ability
of those who represented the United States at
the two Hague Conferences of 1899 and 1907,
the American contributions to the deliberations
and recommendations of those notable assemblies were most important. Indeed, when the
record of history comes to be made up, it may
be that those contributions will be judged to
mark the beginning of a new epoch in the
world's history.

The Conference which now assembles to consider and discuss the international relations
and the international policies of the United
States, is a beginning and only a beginning
of a campaign of education and enlightenment
which is to continue until there has been developed among all parts and sections of our land
what I ventured some years ago to describe as
the "international mind."[1] The international
mind is nothing else than that habit of think-

---

[1] *Cf.* "The International Mind." (New York: Charles Scribner's Sons, 1913.)

ing of foreign relations and business and that habit of dealing with them which regard the several nations of the civilized world as free and co-operating equals in aiding the progress of civilization, in developing commerce and industry, and in spreading enlightenment and culture throughout the world. It would be as inconsistent with the international mind to attempt to steal some other nation's territory or to do that nation an unprovoked injury or damage, as it would be inconsistent with the principles of ordinary morality to attempt to steal some other individual's purse or to commit an unprovoked assault upon him. The international mind requires that a nation and its government shall freely and gladly grant to every other nation and to every other government the rights and the privileges which it claims for itself. From this it follows that the international mind is not consonant with any theory of the State which regards the State as superior to the rules and restrictions of moral conduct or which admits the view that to some one State is committed the hegemony of the world's affairs for the world's good. When that doctrine prevails and takes hold of the conviction and the imagination of a great people, an issue is presented that cannot be settled by vote in conference, that cannot be arbitrated by the wisest statesmen, and that cannot be determined by the findings of any court. The authority and the value of each of these modes of procedure is challenged by the very issue itself. Therefore resort must be had to armed force in order to determine whether the international mind, shared by a score or more of independent and self-respecting nations, shall prevail, or whether the arms of a non-moral, all-powerful, military imperialism shall be stretched out over the whole round world for its government and its protection. It is to determine this issue that the world is now at war.

Should the cause of imperialism, by any chance, win this war, the people of the United States would find it quite unnecessary for some time to come to concern themselves with foreign relations and with foreign policy. Those matters would be taken care of for them by a power that had shown itself strong enough to overcome and to suppress the internationally minded men and nations. On the other hand, if, as we confidently hope and believe, the issue of this war is to be favorable to the free, self-governing democracies of the world, then the people of the United States must address themselves with redoubled energy and with closest attention to those matters of legislation, of administration, and of general public policy which constitute and determine national conduct. The first task of this Conference and of every similar conference that may be held hereafter is to drive this lesson home.

When this task is undertaken it will speedily appear that our government is not well organized at the moment for the formulation and prosecution of effective international policies. The division of authority between the national government and governments of the several States raises one kind of problem. Action under the treaty-making power of the national government raises another set of problems, particularly since there is not yet a substantial unanimity of opinion as to the scope and authority of the treaty-making power itself, or as to the proper and effective means which should be at the command of the government of the United States for enforcing among its own people adherence to a treaty obligation into which, through their government, they have solemnly entered. The difficulties with which we shall have to contend are, therefore, not alone difficulties arising from present lack of popular information and present lack of popular interest in international policies, but they are also those which arise from the structure and the operation of our own form of constitutional government.

That the old secrecy of diplomatic action has gone forever is a happy circumstance. This secrecy was well suited to the making of conventions between ruling monarchs or reigning dynasties, or between governments which represented only very select and highly privileged classes. It has no place, however, in diplomatic intercourse between democratic peoples. The people themselves must understand and assent to international policies and contracts that are entered upon and executed in their name. Otherwise there can be no assurance that these policies will be executed and these contracts observed; for without foreknowledge on the part of the people of that to which they are committed there can be no successful moral appeal made to them to keep their word and their bond at a later time when an opposition may arise between principle and immediate self-interest.

We are assembled, then, to help begin a movement which must not cease until the entire American people are interested in their international relationships, their international position, and their international influence. When that shall have been even measurably accomplished, the people themselves will be quick to bring about such changes in the form of their governmental structure and in their administrative procedure as will enable them honorably and finely to maintain their place, not as a nation that lives to itself alone, but as a nation that shares with every other like-minded nation the desire and the purpose to improve the lot of mankind everywhere, and to carry into the uttermost parts of the earth those hopes, those principles, and those forms of governmental action that are best adapted to giving man the fullest opportunity to make himself free, and to be worthy of freedom.

XVII

A WORLD IN FERMENT

An Address delivered at the 163d Commencement of
Columbia University, June 6, 1917

A WORLD IN FERMENT

The hundreds, indeed the thousands, of American youth who pass out from this University to-day go into a new and a strange world. It is more than a world at war; it is a world in ferment. From the steppes of Russia all the way across Europe and America and around to Japan and China, men and nations are not only engaged in a titanic military struggle but they are also examining and, when necessary, quickly readjusting and reorganizing their customary habits of thought and of action, private as well as public. It is not easy, perhaps it is impossible, to find an Ariadne who will give us a guiding thread through this labyrinth of change. Presuppositions that have long sustained the solid fabric of personal and of national conduct have been destroyed. Assumptions that have seemed to be made certain by the earlier progress of man have disappeared under the pressure of the latest manifestations of trained human capacity for evil.

Before such a scene the timid will despair, while the reckless will affect an indifference that they cannot really feel. The wise will follow a different course. They will not be hurried into judging of normal man on the basis of his latest abnormalities, and they will not permit themselves to forget all that human history teaches because the happenings of the moment seem to teach something quite different. The wise will not lose their sense of proportion in judging of events in time, in space, or in circumstance.

Each individual whose training has really reached the depths of his nature and so has formed his habits of thought and of action, will first examine his own relation to what is going on in the world, and will next inquire how that which is going on is to be judged in terms of everlasting standards of right and of wrong, of progress and of decline. He will first of all find himself to be a member of a politically organized group which is a nation. He will find himself beholden to that group, to its traditions, to its ideals, and to its highest interests, not as a parasite but as a strengthening and a contributing force. Recognition of this relationship will be the basis of his loyalty, and the measure of his loyalty will be not lip-service but sacrifice. He will in this way discover that the ends of which his group or nation is in search are the ends that he must strive to accomplish. It will not be difficult for him to see that in most cases, in the vast majority of cases, these ends are to be reached by persuasion, by argument, by consent, but that in the last resort if they be ends on which turns the whole future of mankind they must, if need be, find protection and defense in physical and military force. This is a sad but significant evidence of the incomplete development of mankind.

He will next apply the standards of moral excellence and approval to the present-day conduct of men and of nations, with a view to determining whether the changes that are going forward are making for human progress or for human decline. He will be led to answer this question by the relative importance accorded to ideas and ideals. If men and nations are engaged in a blind struggle for material gain, for mere conquest, for revenge, or for future privileges, then what is going on is in high degree a manifestation of bestiality in man. If, on the other hand, the struggle be one for the establishment on the largest possible scale, in the securest possible way, of those institutions and opportunities which make man free, then the contest rises to the sublime. In this latter case every contestant on behalf of such a cause is a hero, and every one who offers his life and his strength and his substance is a sincere lover of his kind.

It may therefore well be that it is for the issue of this war to determine whether mankind is still in progress or has begun his decline. If the moral, the economic, and the physical power of men and of nations that love freedom is adequate to its establishment on a secure basis, then mankind is still in progress and new vistas of satisfaction and of accomplishment are to be spread out before him. If, on the other hand, the strength of men and of nations that love freedom is not adequate to this severe task, then man has crossed the Great Divide of his political history and is to begin a descent into those dark places where force and cruelty and despotism wreak their will. Nothing less than this is the alternative which now confronts not alone the nations of the earth, but every individual in each one of those nations. The responsibility for action and for service cannot be devolved upon some one else, least of all can it be devolved upon government officials and government agencies. These have their great part to play, but in last resort the issue will be decided, not by governments, not even by armies and by navies, but by men and women who are the support of all these and whose convictions and stern action are the foundation upon which government and armies and navies rest.

Let there be no faltering by any son or daughter of Columbia. The clock of time is about to strike the most portentous hour in all history. May each child of this ancient University take inspiration and courage from Alma Mater herself, who in her long life has in time of trouble never wavered, in time of danger never hesitated, in time of difficulty never doubted. May all her children be forever worthy of her!

INDEX